"The exploration of the self is an arduous task and one frequently fraught with pain. Zelda Gatuskin is willing to face the pain with the guidance and at times the insistence of her ancestors. Their spirits speak to her through dreams and recorded family history, and she responds with this collection of essays, poetry, stories, drama and collages. With a deceptively simple yet strong voice, she explores and celebrates what it means to be a Jew, to be a woman, and to be a member of the human race. Begun during the Gulf War, her voyage of self-discovery has a broader message from which we can all benefit."

-- Anne Barney
Author of STOLEN JOY:
HEALING AFTER INFERTILITY
AND INFANT LOSS

"The book is a poetical tribute to the psyche, ancestors, buried myths of family, friend and enemy alike. The author soul searches forward and backward, see-sawing the reader through her explorations. This is an important step in her career as a writer and a reward to those who discover it for themselves."

-- Gerald Hausman
Author of TURTLE ISLAND ALPHABET
and TUNKASHILA

ANCESTRAL NOTES

A Family Dream Journal

Zelda Leah Gatuskin

Illustrated by the Author

Printed in the United States of America
        First Printing, 1994
        ISBN: 0-938513-17-6
        L.I.C.# 94-70776

AMADOR PUBLISHERS
P. O. Box 12335
Albuquerque, NM 87195 USA

for my sisters

Acknowledgements

The tongue I am of those who lived before me, as those that are to come will be the voice of my unspoken thoughts. And so who shall be applauded if the song be sweet, if the prophecy be true?

Mary Antin
THE PROMISED LAND, 1912

The process of compiling these ANCESTRAL NOTES was an immersion into murky waters. My sincerest thanks to all of you who were with me on this journey; you who kept me from drowning, who provided me with the tools and gave me the courage to keep plunging deeper.

Zelda Leah Gatuskin, 1994

About The Illustrations

I have been expressing myself as a visual artist for many more years than as a writer. When it was suggested that I illustrate ANCESTRAL NOTES with my own collages, I realized that I had already tackled much of this subject matter from a graphic perspective. The focus of my collage work over the past five years has been to interpret graphically the experience of dreams. Prior to this inquiry, I was exploring the possibilities of making social/political statements through the ironic juxtaposition of images. In ANCESTRAL NOTES, these two themes converge: dreams serve as the point of connection between myself and my ancestral spirits, who then demand a statement of solidarity between past and future in recognition of the universal and timeless struggles of humanity. The collages contained within, while created specifically for this work, are nonetheless extensions of previous efforts. Dreams serve as the launching point, juxtaposed contemporary images as the vehicle.

ANCESTRAL NOTES is not an historical document, but the chronicle of a personal awakening. The family stories recounted here are freely fictionalized, and I have avoided using the real names of the people on whom they are based just as I have purposefully excluded our actual family photos from use as illustrations. It is my hope that readers will mentally illustrate my stories with faces and places from their own family albums, while using the collages provided as a doorway into their own dreams.

Table Of Illustrations

CONTENTS

Introduction — The War Is On TV

January 17, 1991

The war is on TV. What a show. Col. Sam Dickens, US Air Force (ret.) and Gen. Edward Meyer (former army chief of staff) take calls and chat with Larry King on CNN during lulls in the bombing. Richard Roth, reporting from Tel Aviv, likes to refer to Israel as "the Jewish State." Is he some kind of militant Zionist, posing as respectable CNN reporter? Or is he just tactfully reminding us that the reason Israel is Saddam Hussein's first and favorite target is that it is the Jewish State? This brings up a lot of old stuff for me... Ancient stuff. Millennia old.

How can humans have such short memories and yet such long memories? I was watching the kids march down and up Central Avenue today protesting the war. Huhm! What do they know about marching? I marched. At the tender age of thirteen I marched down Pennsylvania Avenue to express my conviction that war is wrong; war is always wrong. I knew a very little about Vietnam. I know a little more now. Thanks to TV, I know a lot more about what's going on in Iraq and Kuwait. But it doesn't matter about the details when you know, you just know, that all war is wrong, all killing is wrong, all lying is wrong, that letting people starve and live in the streets is wrong... I watched the kids marching down and up Central. They were not all kids.

1

Dan Rather is "letting roll" the first pictures out of Tel Aviv tonight. The bombed-out neighborhood is panned and we are assured that the casualties have been very light. The camera lingers over the white feathered corpse of a chicken. This is followed by headlines nicely encapsulating tonight's news:

IRAQI MISSILES HAVE HIT ISRAEL
ISRAEL HAS NOT RETALIATED
PRESIDENT BUSH IS OUTRAGED

Oh, our memories are so short and so long. One day I was wearing patched bell bottoms and a tee shirt emblazoned with the word PEACE as I was rocked and rolled along Pennsylvania Avenue in a mash of fully integrated humanity, all of us knowing, **knowing**, what was right and what was wrong and what would never happen again once **we** entered the inner sanctums of power. But then we forgot; I forgot. I got busy growing up, going to college, falling in love, working, making art, dancing... I forgot. Twenty years have gone by and the kids marching down and up Central make me almost remember, but it seems so long ago. What should I have been remembering these twenty years? What was it we were supposed to do? I can't remember. I just know we didn't do it.

Only my long memory is functioning now. The one that creeps back into the genes. The old long memory of life sweetened by threat. A memory that says there are things worth dying for, and sometimes you have to lie and steal and cheat, too. "It's survival," the memory says, "it's **us**." And I see my ancestors stretching back and back through time, all of our ancestors. A long chain of dead souls, generation after generation, linked arm to arm, reaching toward us - the living, the present - while our long arm-to-arm chain reaches into the future, pulls away from them... But eventually we all die, and fall back into their arms gratefully and gather ourselves up and take our place in their chain and reach, reach out to the living saying, "Remember, remember..."

"We spin along," my ancestors remind me, "and lucky we do. Look at all of us — only in Zion might we all walk the earth together."

In Zion, in Israel. In Palestine. Oh, these are old, old memories. The memories that wars are made of.

January 17, 1994

This is where ANCESTRAL NOTES started, with the Persian Gulf War. It made something snap. It was like that recurring dream I have, where I suddenly realize I have not been attending classes for a certain subject and I now have to take the exam. I'd had a lot of questions when I was younger, about family, religion, and society, about war, peace, and politics. Some of them were just too hard or too painful; some actually seemed irrelevant. The war woke me up. I really had been skipping class for about twenty years...

A week into the Gulf War, Harry Willson of Amador Publishers called to express interest in a novel I had written. By March, THE TIME DANCER was on its way to publication and I had adopted a new last name, Gatuskin. That is, I had decided to reclaim a family name from three generations back and put it in print on the cover of a book. My hope was (and is) that some long-lost relative might find me and tell me about the mysterious Gatuskin line. I had by then already started dabbling in genealogical research.

Now my folks were doubly pleased; I had become an author **and** taken an interest in the family history. My grandmother said, "You have taken the name of a very fine man, and I know he's up there somewhere smiling down at you." I knew that too. And as I delved further into all branches of the family, I began to sense the presence of an entire array of ancestral spirits. As I charted their names and read about the places and times in which they lived, as I pumped relatives for memories and information, their voices began to speak to me and through me.

Still, I do not know if it was really I who summoned these
spirits, or the times. The Gulf War came and went, leaving tens
of thousands of brown-skinned people dead. Forget romanticism
about Israel, forget the flag-waving, yellow-ribboned patriotism
of the victors; this looked like genocide to me. Then, a year
later, an "orphan bus" screamed across the headlines. It was
carrying children out of war-torn Sarajevo. Today, that city
bears some striking similarities to the Warsaw Ghetto. This was
how we celebrated the fiftieth anniversary of World War II, with
"racial cleansing" in the Balkans.

This past year has brought Israel and its Arab neighbors into
the headlines again. An historic handshake, a promise of peace
— while at every juncture one group or another, or all, beat the
old refrains of hostility and mistrust. As of this writing, peace
in the Middle East remains elusive; war still rages in Bosnia.
Racial hatred is prevalent throughout the world, familiar as an
old friend and as hard to cast out. Here at home, we have
recently learned of our own country's unconscionable human
experiments with plutonium in the aftermath of World War II;
our neighborhoods are plagued by violence; and an earthquake
in Los Angeles this very day reminds us of how tenuous is the
security we take for granted.

Surely the ancestors have always been with me, as have
been the threats and heartaches that often seem far removed from
the life of comfort I am so privileged to lead. I had only to
sleep, to dream, then to wake to recognition of my inheritance.
ANCESTRAL NOTES, the book, has reached its conclusion, but
the process is ongoing. Every dire headline resonates with
lessons from the past and implications for the future. I make my
way through a world of accelerating change with the weight of
an ancestral hand on my shoulder. It comforts, it prods, it grips.
Whenever I feel small and alone and unable to make sense of
life's convulsions, it draws me back through the classrooms,
libraries and museums of my dreams, to the textbook of genetic
memory. From the shadowy late-night lectures of ancestral
spirits spring surprising moments of clarity.

PART I

The Dream Library

I Want To Live In My Dreams

I want to live in my dreams
I want to visit those labyrinthine halls by day
To taste, at last, those breads and cakes and pastries
Prepared in my nocturnal cafeteria
Located within the bowels of that great
Mall/museum/classroom/auditorium/apartment complex complex
Which also sometimes serves as
Airport/train-station/subway/bus-terminal
It's a terminal complex
Where the deceased are as likely to be among the arrivals
And departures as the dreaming
Certainly I have taken the wrong train often enough
In my dreams
Missed the lecture, the opening act
Lost the invitation
Failed to comprehend in so many ways
Frustrating the writer/director/producer of my dreams
Into something shamefully lacking in subtlety
Such as English words literally written out for me on the walls
Of my block-brained head
Snotty, ironic dream graffiti
Like, "You can forget the cosmic message"
Suggesting I am just too dense to be worthy of the detoured
Journey I both fear and want
I run all night without covering new ground

I rush and rush but never get there any faster
In this dream

Here is the thing about dreams:
A nasty moment can be drawn out for a long time
And become the total reality
The bathroom door won't close...won't close...won't close...
My skirt is falling down...falling down...falling down...
The dog is biting me...biting me...biting me...
The bus won't stop to me let me off...let me off...
LET ME OFF!
And you think I'm crazy to want to live in a world such as this
But I do, I do want to live in my dreams
Where I get to have a rotten, paranoid time
And just keep having it until I've got it out of my system
Without apologies
Or excessive analysis
Or self-recriminations ruining the fun scenes
Just the opposite of this so-called real existence
Where such primal, fearful, humiliating events
Rarely do take place
Yet I torment myself worrying how to prevent them
My waking world is predictable, orderly, and controllable
Left-brained, linear
Which makes me fear I'll fail to fulfill my rational role here
Creating this constant anxiety to stay on track

At least things are allowed to go amiss in dreams
Dreams are fueled by the unexpected
The gravity of dreams is moon-like
And matter is often immaterial
I fly in my dreams
I have only to raise my arms
For the ground to drop away below me
I can bounce high into the air
Or glide low within the confines of dream chambers

With my limbs all wavy and thin like a Chagall painting
Anything is possible
A touch, a smile
Moments more erotic than flesh will ever know...
I want to live in my dreams
Where I can turn a corner onto a whole new scene
To holiday at the cottage by the river
Where flotillas of hot air balloons migrate downstream
Alight to pluck us from a river wade
And lift us above the lazy leafy canopy

You think I'm spacey enough already
Without having to live in my dreams
But this is just the problem
Too much space
It is so hard to make connections in this waking world
In my dreams there is no space
No distance
I know your thoughts
I think them for you
I am in your face
Always exactly who I am
No matter what mask I wear

Yes, I want to live in my dreams
And make objects levitate
And bathe in a guitar case
And audition to be in the audience
And travel the high road led by an ancestral crone
And dance in slow motion on shoes with brush bristle soles
And paint portraits that come to life
And do everything twice
And do everything twice
And smile upon myself and my universe with the beatific visage
Of sleeping Vishnu
Dreaming a lotus blossom out of his *pupik*

So Close

They are so close to me now,
These ancestors.
I can almost feel the moist wind of their spirit breath,
If there is such a thing.
Or maybe it is the breeze from their spirit wings
That brushes my forehead as I awake,
Groggy and confused
From dreams so complex, so layered,
They cannot be described.
And even as I move through the day
I will occasionally glimpse a special light
That casts all in such a dreamlike quality
I must suspect the presence of ghosts;
And that my view is altered by their ethereal prism.

There is a dream I have been trying to remember...
(I have been wanting to remember it for about twenty-five years)
Can I ever hope to know it now
Or just to make it up?
(My imagination being so much sharper than my memory)
I dare not settle on a single image, to admit to any one event
Lest I scare the truth away in my rush to fill in the blanks.
Patience.

This dream is in there somewhere;
I sense it like a mote on the edge of my vision.

I think I'll know it when I see it,
Though I know so little of it now.
I think I'll know it when I feel it.
And every so often I do feel the atmosphere of this dream
And see the dream light;
And those moments coincide with the light-shadows
Of spirits crossing before my eyes.
A whole lifetime was lived in that dream,
Possibly many.
If so, there is not enough time in this life to know.
But, patience.
There are plenty of other dreams through which to browse
Here in the dream library...

Death Is A Wall

Dream Journal Entry

I had been reading about dreams, sleep, etc. Hillman said dreams have only to do with death. Because we can't deal with death when waking, we have to dream about it. I started thinking about death — trying to focus my waking mind on it and deal with whatever emotions came up. I had this dream:

Death was a wall. That is, a wall separated Life and Death. I determined to look over the wall to see Death. I could not climb the wall. When I was physically able to reach the top, my will would fail and I'd fall back. I was determined to conquer my fear and scale the wall — I had to face Death. After more unsuccessful attempts I stepped back and considered again:

Death is a wall.

I could not look at it without passing through it. With that realization I walked forward without fear and passed through the wall without effort; at that moment I woke.

After having that dream, I stopped troubling myself (for the time) about Death.

Death Is A Wall

The Museum Of Pain And Suffering

Dream Journal Entries

A Boston-like setting (Back Bay). There is a new museum which has just opened: THE MUSEUM OF PAIN AND SUFFERING. It is in a large brownstone set back from the street with a wrought iron fence around its little yard and a big banner hanging from the fence: THE MUSEUM OF PAIN AND SUFFERING. I have no intention of going in! But I keep finding this museum — it seems to have an entrance on every side of its block. Each time I see its banner, THE MUSEUM OF PAIN AND SUFFERING, I reaffirm to myself that I don't want to go in — "I know what's in there."

I was given a family album and when I opened it I found photographs of graves and not of people...

I am in an elevator — very large with about six to eight others and an elevator operator. "The ride down will take **four days**," he says. There is no other way out of wherever we are. I notice a second set of doors which I hope leads to a bathroom — I become sick feeling (almost nausea, that dropping stomach feeling) as soon as the elevator starts to move. I have no confidence that I can survive the trip either mentally or physically.

14

The Spirit Floats

The body is wet and the spirit is dry:
Sea foam washes over sand
Physical sensations wash away small glimpses of eternity

To have one's spirits dampened
Is to have them weighed down
The spirit is meant to float and sometimes fly
The body is wet and the spirit is dry

* * *

One night as I slept, flat on my back, head turned to the left:

A large palm was placed firmly on my left cheek
and lifted my head back to center
with a force that woke me
And there I lay, staring straight up at the ceiling
in a room empty but for me
and quiet but for my heart
I was twelve then, and I was sure at the time
as I am now
that the hand was that of a spirit
The spirit was warning me
not to look over my left shoulder
to the place where the mysteries are

My neck has gotten stiff over the years
from the strain of not looking for the spirits
Lately, I think the spirits are ready to visit with **me**
This time I will know who they are
I will recognize them as the ghosts of my ancestors
and the mysteries as their memories
I look over my shoulder
not only to a spirit place that cannot be seen
but literally to the past
To that which is behind me

Now I lie in bed, flat on my back with my head turned to the
left, and my left hand levitates — relaxed, warm, floating...

A spirit is holding my hand

* * *

In my dream there were two of me:

My dream self was awake, and my waking self was asleep
My dream self wanted to be dry, to lighten the spirit
My waking self wanted to sleep, to free the spirit
The water bearer offered water to us both

I knew that once my waking self was sleeping comfortably
my dream self would speak to the water bearer
But when I put my sleeping waking self to bed
my waking dream self slipped in as well
and we became one being
A sleeping waking dreamless dream being

* * *

I have now been visited twice in as many days
By ancestral spirits
They have a message for me:

The body is wet and the spirit is dry
When life is good, let the body be wet
Soak up the goodness of the earth
Enjoy moist sensations
Celebrate creation

But when life is bad and the only sensation is pain
And the energies of the earth and humankind are full of
Destruction

Remember that the spirit is dry
It floats, and sometimes it flies

Soap For Bones

In the desert, the air cools quickly after sunset.
We hug ourselves and watch the moon rise,
A sliver of bone in the black brew of the night sky.
And the cold does not make us shiver so much
As the rattling of our bone memories.
We build a fire and sink to the ground beside it
To listen to the ancient stories of that old potsherd,
That old bone relic of a moon.

For how many thousands of years
Has a bone been thrown into a pot
And the pot filled with water and the water boiled
So that humans might be fed?
Too many to count.
Count instead the tools of human survival:
Soup pot, water, fire, drum, and bone.

"Oh sliver of moon, sliver of bone,
Tell again the story of how a soup pot
Became the first drum
Which was beaten with a bone bound in hide.
Or how the soup pot itself
Was first fashioned from water and clay,
Baked in hot coals and then lifted from the fire-pit
On the knob of a shankbone.

Or share with us stories of the seas
And how their briny swells lift up to meet you
As you cast your splinters of bone down upon their waves.
By night these skeletons float and flicker white.
With daylight they settle within the deep wet grave,
Taking with them your moon mysteries,
Perhaps someday to be found churned up upon the shore
Tamed by tumbled sand."

Such are the liquid visions of the desert tribes
As we rest upon our infinite beach.
But a cloud crosses between us and our moon-window,
Our peephole in the night's door.
And the spotlight is shifted away from these bone memories
While vapor shadows instead breathe bone prophecy to life:

City dwellers we will be
Our moon will grow distant, our fires timid, our drums muted
Our beliefs will be bound up in books
And our worship entombed in buildings of brick
But the soup pot will still burble with the life force
And the quest to fill our stomachs will bind us to All beings
As surely as the quest to fill this lonely expanse of intellect
Will ever propel us toward the One being
City dwellers we will be
Our moon will grow distant, our fires timid, our drums muted
But the soup pot will still burble with the life force...

"Bones for soup? Bones for soup?"
Unable to afford meat, we go to the butcher for bones. Marrow
to marrow, we draw life from death. From the bones of cattle
and sheep and fowl generations are nourished. And when every
last nutrient has been boiled into soup, the bones' work is still
not done...

"Bones for soap! Bones for soap!"
The soap peddlers call as they wind through narrow tenement
streets. "Bones for soap!" And we hand over our soup bones
in exchange for bars of smelly, yellow carbolic soap. So that on
Mondays we replace our soup pots with the big vats in which we
boil laundry; and the pungent smell of shirt soup replaces the
aromas of broth and stew.

Bones for soap. Soap for bones.
Yet the bones of our human dead are forever unclean. Once the
spirit has left the body the worth of our bones is spent. Neither
nourished nor nourishing. Neither cleansed nor cleansing. A
visit to the cemetery must be followed by the ritual washing of
hands.   On the sidewalk, before entering the house, the
uncleanliness of the dead is left behind. The water that has been
poured over the hands of the mourners trickles into the gutters,
flows to the rivers, flows to the sea, purifying itself.

Bones for soap. Bones for soup.
Such simplicity, such innocence...
Until, one day, it is our own bones made into soap, our own
flesh made into candles. Our hordes become herds, harvested
like cattle. Now we are truly one with all of God's creatures for
there is no burden we have not borne.
Who washes with our bones?
Who lights his way with our flesh?

It will be a dreary passage
                    And when the flame sputters and dies
                              Stand with us in the void
                                    And consider
                                          Bones

A mountain of bones
A mountain of bones
White and sparkling in the sun
Dry, cracking, flaking
A virtual
Tower of
Babel of
Bones
Picked over and squabbled over
Then bashed into sand, ground into white powder
And borne away on a hot wind to stick like a bonemeal mask
To the sweaty face of history

A pit of bones
A pit of bones
Still white
Still and white
White within black
When the last clod of earth falls on the open grave
and moist dark soil closes in around them, do the bones yet glow
White?

Do they whisper still the parched secrets of the dry spirit?
Do they stay aloof from the churning organic, orgasmic
gyrations of earth guts
ever dry and white and brittle like Wild West
Bones?

Probably not, not our pit of bones bones
They will turn to glue and maggot food and no matter how
thoroughly we wash our hands when we leave the graveside
Traces of bone slime will linger
A prophecy memorized by genes and retold by ghosts
The pit devours but it does not forget

An ocean of bones
An ocean of bones
Is not the sea a giant grave and at the same time
The place where all life originated?
Is not the seashell the forerunner of the bone?
Was not Lot's wife turned into a pillar of salt
And ultimately washed into the Sea
Where the curious dine on a porridge of water, salt and bones?

A broth of bones
A broth of bones
The food of the life force
Enemy to all disease
When we dine on soup we renew our essential components:
Moisture, heat, marrow, meat
Bone spirit, earth spirit, bone spirit, ocean spirit
So what is as important to good health as good nourishment?
Cleanliness

But a bath of bones?
A bath of bones?
Like the tallow itself
Truth
Slips and slides and melts away into
Nothing
Purity and evil
Life and death
Solid, liquid and
Gas
Foam together like so much suds
Now that we have bathed to our last lung-searing breath
In a chamber of fear
In our own
Bath of bones

Bones for soap
Soap for bones

Ghostly silent, the cloud trails float aside
And with them this anxious prescience.
Moon is back, but this time we stand and curse it:
"Come, let us pick a bone with you!
And tell us now, if it be a righteous bone
Or a repugnant bone?
A living, life-giving bone, or one dead and rotting?
Moon splinters indeed!
This desert sand is nothing but bone dust.
And from one end of the earth to the other,
From one end of time to the other,
The **sun** rises and sets in pools of blood!"
We shake our bony fists at the descending moon,
"Ha ha! Ha ha!"

From One End Of Time To The Other

Germany

Germany
Germany
Germany
Germany
Germany
Does not the story of the Eastern European Jew begin and end
With Germany?

The end we all know
Flight or death
Conversion, subversion, internment
After that, who could be German?

So you are
Lithuanian, Hungarian, Russian, Polish, French, Italian
But I ask you:
Go back a few more generations with me
Will we meet
In Germany?

Am I not something of a philosopher?
Compulsively organized?
Loyal?
Law abiding?
Clever?
Whose traits are these?

I heard myself make a racist remark
About Germans
It surprised me
And then I knew
That was me too

We are like southern belles
Who blanch at the suggestion that the blood of slaves
Courses through their veins
Can you say Denial in Yiddish?
Say it in German, that's close enough

Faval's Vision

It was Faval; I know it was Faval; Faval who sat rigid in a straight-backed wooden chair with his hands resting on his thighs, his skin pale, his frame gaunt, his eyes and hair soft and dark brown. It was Faval in his twenties, and but for being an adult, he appeared exactly as I have always imagined him as a boy of five: seated in a straight-backed wooden chair, in a poorly lit house, watching the front door and, through it, the ghost of his father fighting back Polish police. Perhaps I was only five years old myself when I was first told the story of Faval's vision by my grandmother, his older half-sister. Because Faval's boyhood vision is a family legend of a magical event:

The police did come to the house that night - so the story goes - looking for young men to draft into the army. But they found none. For Faval had told his vision to his mother and she had understood her late husband's message and sent all the elder sons away to hide.

Still, this story of Faval's vision is not one of victory but of ultimate defeat. It is always told with a shake of the head and a sigh for the young Faval, the favored one, the love child, descendent of Rabbis and magistrates, graced with the eyes of a prophet; Faval who carried in his veins the promises of generations past, the refinement of every gene of intellect and inspiration and beauty, and yet was destined to waste away within the walls of Warsaw until... until...

Faval himself finally appeared as an adult to tell me the truth, which only he may tell. Because he was the youngest,

27

he saw things as they were, saw the danger lurking sooner than the others, saw the need to fight, raised the alarm; Faval and his young friends, the ones who were born into war, who had no memories of countrysides and friendly townspeople, of elbow room and hope. Yes, fifty years later, Faval himself showed up in a dream to tell me exactly how the Nazis killed him and his family (our family). "Gassed us." He told it to my companion more than to me, as if he couldn't fully face me. (But it was my dream; I was the one who couldn't fully face him.) "Gassed us." And acting as dream editor, I censored the message and penned a last name, G-A-U-S-T-A-U-S, which on waking I also duly documented, thinking this was connected to the name "Gatuskin." But, as the day went by, I kept hearing him say it (he, who could only be Faval). "Gassed us; gassed us; they gassed us." He wouldn't have felt he had to tell me his name. I was supposed to recognize him from his posture, from the straight-backed chair and the wide eyes. (I have always seen his eyes, his eyes watching the door, and beyond it - through it - the ghost of his father...) It was Faval, of course. After the dream, I had the nerve to ask specifically about the circum-stances of their deaths (but not before first asking for the story of Faval's vision just once more). "Gassed."

All of them, my grandmother continued, the whole family, while trying to escape from the Warsaw Ghetto; "gassed in the underground." (I count the names on my chart, the names that do not have "Paris," "U.S.," "London," "Israel" penned after them; I count twenty-five names.) The shake of the head, the sigh, the defeat, stopped me from asking more. So I read; how and when would they have been trying to escape? What exactly was the "underground?" I read; and I wonder again about Faval; and a new vision emerges of him.

He does not sit. He is busy, he and his friends who know nothing of freedom or fat. It is they themselves who are the underground, they and the resistance inside and outside the Ghetto; and the goal is to get from the inside to the outside and then from the outside to Russia and there to join with the bigger movements for relief and resistance. So the underground becomes a physical thing as well, a maze of cellars, sewer lines, sealed-in rooms, and tunnels, tunnels; tunnels that push their way to the very walls of the Ghetto, and below... and out! Faval does not sit. He connives, he cajoles, he reconnoiters; he convinces his family that they are doomed if they stay and it is his own rank among the resisters that wins them their chance through the tunnel.

Now, fifty years later, Faval may again sit, in a straight-backed wooden chair, with his hands on his knees and his brown eyes wide and his jaw set. Only now it is **my** vision; I will him to tell more and myself to listen:

"Gassed us. And I led the way; I and my young friends who knew nothing of green grass, for whom walls and tunnels and cellars and locked rooms were our playgrounds and hide-and-seek was a game of life and death. Deep into the thing, with the Ghetto burning to the ground above us, and we the very last desperate survivors scrambling through our tunnels and bunkers, waiting for some sign that we might move on, I saw him again. In the hidden room, atop the grate in the floor, my father wrestled with the soldiers of the SS. But he could not save us this time; we were trapped. They let the gas in slowly so we might suffer longer while we died."

Now I know why my grandmother believes that Hitler lives still in Hell, forever tortuously dying, forbidden the respite of death. He is allowed to die only so that he can be brought back to life again to experience yet more agony; millions and millions of deaths must he suffer as punishment for those he wrought.

And Faval sits enthroned in Heaven, on a straight-backed wooden chair, a stern guardian angel. He teaches me that to have a vision is not enough; one must act swiftly and with faith. Once I closed my eyes and tried to conjure him for inspiration, to which he said: "Do not set aside your pen. Dreams are the flimsy stuff of ghosts, but in your works we live again."

Taking The Sword

Dream Journal Entries

(the end of a fable...) "And hearing of her plight, the queen gave her letters so she could name her pain."

The usual multi-storied, labyrinthine house/apartment complex. I am on an upper floor. Mom appears at the window. She has scaled the buttress to peek in and tell me something about a sword. I rush down and around to the yard. Mom is waiting for me on a bench. We sit there and talk and look over to where she had climbed up to the window. There is a sword on the ground. We go and get it.

Last night, my dreams took me down into the foundations of a house. I was the assistant to a priestess who wore black robes. We descended a wooden stairway. Moist sand thinly coated the steps, accumulating in thick piles in the corners of the stairs. I stopped to shape these mounds into tall, thin pillars which could only be built so high before crumbling against my palms. Then I joined the priestess at a large table at the base of the stairs. Many spirits were gathered around. Beyond us, square wooden beams partitioned the vast cellar into a maze of rooms; and every room was full of books.

Shadows

How to remember a dream that was never remembered
Even once?
And why?
This dream being just one of many into which I am immersed
While sleeping,
But evaporates instantly into the air
On waking,
When I feel like I have read the last sentence of a book
Only to forget every word that came before.
The agony of all that effort wasted, all that learning...
There is nothing to do but pick the book up once more,
The next evening,
And start afresh.
But of all the books on the shelves of the dream library,
I cannot pick this one out.
I've held a thousand others; and some I even remember,
Or at least have come to recognize,
Having returned to them again and again.
But this dream must be in another section...

Is there a children's room in this library?
And if so, can I get there from here?
At what age was this dream dreamt?

I am walking back through the book-lined corridors
Of the dream library.

To left and right, the rooms of the places I have lived;
And straight ahead, but far,
Far down the long hallway,
Beyond the foot of the stairs,
The playroom.
Something catches my eye...
A certain book?
I cannot really see it.
It shimmers,
Not quite a mirage,
Too out of focus...
I sense sunshine, pale blue skies, green hills,
A baby's dream, in coloring book formation,
Blocks of color, no details.
Into the playroom now:
See how the light changes
When a cloud crosses the sun.
And now I do remember that when I was four
I watched for what seemed like hours
As shadows fell across a framed picture on the wall,
And the scene shifted from warmly glowing
To coldly stark.
Yet I can remember no more of the subject of that picture
Than I can of this scrap of dream!
Only a poignancy, a melancholy,
That deepened with the shadow, lifted with the intensifying sun.
And the moody waves of light made the picture ache and pulse
With precarious promise.
This is how The Dream makes me feel,
The dream I can't,
Or won't,
But must,
Remember.

My Problems

They came to me again last night. I was despondent, could find nothing pleasing about myself at all, and was angry about the War, which was keeping me glued to the TV. So my ancestral spirits, who are becoming increasingly familiar, helpfully reminded me that I was lucky to have the problems I have and not the problems they had:

"Well, that's pretty obvious. I'm not exactly fighting for my very life."

"But knowing this doesn't comfort you."

"It just makes me feel miserable **and** petty."

*"People will always find something to complain about, no matter how much they have to be thankful for. That's just human nature. Be **glad** you are not waking up every day wondering what you can find to eat."*

"Oh, but that's what I am thinking about every day. Food is inordinately important to me. My life is built around meals, my relationships too. Every celebration involves a meal and every consolation demands a snack. This is one of my **big** problems. I feel compelled to consume well beyond my need, even my desire. There's a little hungry deprived child inside me who can never get enough."

"I don't like the sound of that."

"Are you talking about us?"

"Your problems are our fault?"

"Well, food rituals do play a central role in our culture.

The first rules I ever learned and the first rules I ever broke were about food. Plus, times of hunger have a way of lingering in the collective memory. If my comforts are compensation for your hardships, then, yes, you all do play a part in my 'issues' about eating."

"You have 'issues;' we had crises!"

"Maybe the connection is that I get to have all of the problems you **didn't**. Too much food. It's almost funny."

"Better to laugh than cry."

"But I cry, too. That's another problem. I get so emotional, take everything so personally. The news frequently makes me cry. It all seems hopeless. I don't feel like I can fix anything. And I feel like I have to be prepared for my world to collapse at any minute. It would be dangerous to get too comfortable, too complacent. I need to be tough. Horrible things happen every day to innocent people - crime, natural disaster - it takes so little for me to put myself in the victims' shoes. Other people's pain is vivid to me, almost familiar."

"There's that note of accusation again. As if we did this to you, or are doing it to you."

"Your experiences, your memories, color my perceptions. It's only a matter of time before someone identifies the gene marker for pain and grief. I know there is one, the way the tears well up from nowhere at the oddest times. In addition to which, you spirits seem to have the means to intervene directly. Do you think I don't catch the distortion of your ghostly wavelengths? That I haven't followed the clues you plant in my dreams? This dream I can't remember... I think it has to do with some of you, something frightening that happened in the countryside, or was it a desert? Do you want me to know, or don't you? Are you trying to show it to me or hide it?"

"The details are not important. And what's to cry about now? And what's to be afraid of? We are just spirits of the dead. Our pain is past."

"Rest assured that you will never face such inhumanity as we have. The worst has happened, this is what we are here to

tell you.   All of the cruelest, incomprehensibly vile, and malicious acts that can be invented by the human imagination have not only been conceived, but have been born into the world."

"Our deaths are testimony to this, and we give you our memories to free you from fear."

"Thanks a lot. Just what I need, a scorecard of oppression. Something I can wave around while saying, 'Sorry, I'm exempt; my people already paid their dues; bad fortune will just have to fall on someone else this generation...'"

"You don't have to use that tone with us."

"Tell me, do you really know something about the future, or are you just trying to make me feel better? How do you know **my** life won't be interrupted by some cataclysm?"

"Let's just say that suffering you do not have to rehearse. The suffering will come naturally, don't worry about that."

"Whatever happens, you can face the world knowing that there is nothing to lose. This is how we would have faced the world, had we survived."

"That does not answer my question."

"Your question is impossible to answer. Ask another one."

"You say the worst has already happened, and there is nothing for me to be afraid of, so I ask you, why do we keep dwelling on these memories? Why this litany of 'lest it happen again?' For what cause must I face the world?"

"Lest it happen again..."

"...you need not fear being the victim..."

"...but you could find yourself the perpetrator."

"Now that's scary."

"So stop sulking and do something."

"Like what?"

"Pick up the sword."

Taking The Sword

Saving The World

Why the sword? Must I really wield my words like a weapon, threatening thought into submission? Can this one lonely sword slash through all of the muddle and confusion around me?

I have been trying to write this manifesto, on behalf of the spirits, on and off for many months. They demand I make a public protest against the wrongs of the world. As if my words hold some magic power to set everyone aright. But the more fervently I've labored over my tirade, the less I've found to recommend my views above any others. Does my despair really contribute constructively to the dialogue? I have nothing else to share, just a few observations, some clever metaphors, nothing that actually suggests an answer. If anything, I hear in my own voice the dogmatic, know-it-all tones that limit understanding. I practice with the sword by dicing up my treatise into little pieces. If nothing else, I can at least pierce the smooth, easy flow of words which disguises the jagged landscape of thought, like a blanket over a bed of nails.

The blade is sharp, precise; it must have some further use. I find myself using it to probe my own insides. Self-dissection. I am looking to see which attitudes are benign and which are malignant. I am excising the scar tissue that impedes growth. I am literally "spilling my guts" in the classic artistic sacrificial rite. If enough of us put our entrails out for view, will we finally make the point that every creature springs from the same gelatinous goop? That we are all equally vulnerable? That one diseased cell could kill the entire organism?

I keep falling back on dreams and ancestral memories to help me make my political points. Actual, contemporary events are only neutralized by my writing. Abstracted, they turn into symbols, become more digestible; and this is **not** my intent.

The story goes that there is a train of garbage chugging through state after state, and each state refuses to accept the load. No one wants to deal with it, except to maybe tack on another car of trash. "While you're up..." And the train just gets longer. Soon it will have no beginning and no end. Already no one remembers whose garbage it is; but we all agree that it isn't "ours" and shouldn't stop "here." Perfect. Our restless train of garbage snakes across a land that used to seem large enough to hold us all and all our stuff as well. Now, the only way we all fit is if we keep moving, like a game of musical chairs. The Garbage Train never stops. "Hey, hold this for me. See ya later. Bye."

The train of garbage is a tragedy; but what have I done about it? Not much. I recycle a bit more, buy more bulk foods. Mainly, though, the imagery is so strong that I've simply adopted the Garbage Train as my personal metaphor for everything that makes me mad, but I feel powerless to change. It moves ceaselessly, a roving circuit of the mind, and I toss my troubled and troublesome thoughts onto it as it makes an occasional pass through consciousness. Every news report brings more hazardous material to my Garbage Train. I can't keep up. One of these days, the train of garbage will turn into a snake biting its own tail. There'll be no getting away from it.

> I dream I've gotten on the wrong train, going the wrong direction. I wake up. I dream again and I'm back where I started, waiting at the same wrong platform, getting onto the same wrong train, going in the same wrong direction. I wake up. The newspaper is still full of war, starvation, rape, murder and the destruction of the planet.

The problems of our society are stuck to each other like yesterday's coffee grounds to the day-before's plastic bags. What was that the politician said about just rolling up our shirtsleeves? Even if we were willing to get our hands dirty, the job would be overwhelming. Better to package things up in tidy little symbols that we can move around neatly. See how much mileage I get out of the Garbage Train analogy? But the **fact** of the train of garbage remains, along with the facts of all of the other outrages roaming the tracks of my guilty conscience. Naming the problems doesn't solve them.

> Trash moves slowly compared to war. Who knows? Maybe enough people will get killed in wars and because of wars, our trash problems will diminish. There's always a war going on someplace. But wars

in other places are private little matters.   Like disease and starvation, they wipe out entire family groups, entire communities, yet seem to have no wide-reaching effects.   We prefer not to get involved.   (After all, there has to be some mechanism for thinning out the population; better them than us...)

It took a media-hyped "Orphan Bus" full of babies and children for the world to finally acknowledge the race war in Bosnia. We respond to children. Unfortunately, for all of our good intentions, we generally only succeed in creating more neutralized symbols — in this case, darling innocent symbols of everything we need to fight for.

If we could just see children for who they really are and what they really need, I think we would have to stop fighting.

The Orphan Bus is a ready-made metaphor. Such a vivid image, the Orphan Bus: every bit as noisy and smelly as the Garbage Train, but moving at break-neck speed through bombed-out streets, racing maniacally to a safe port where it drops off one load of world children after another.   It plays like a movie across the mind's teary eye; and it seems easy to write in a dramatic, **distant** finale.   But the Orphan Bus is coming **our** way. Sooner or later it **will** stop at our doorstep, leaving us its hungry, hurt and haunted youngsters. What will we do then?

Buses and trains are such provocative images for me. My worst dreams have to do with transpor- tation. Typically, I am on the wrong train or bus, going the wrong direction, through unknown, threatening territory where I wouldn't want to be dropped off even if I **could** get the driver to stop. Often, I have left something or someone behind and/or am separated from my companions/ belongings in the course of my ride. Am I too concerned with "getting somewhere," "going places?" Is this the nightmare of a "control freak?" It's true I hate to lose things, especially myself. I cling to the notion that there is a preferred destination, that movement is toward or away from a given point, that there is such a thing as "progress."

The terror of being on the wrong train, going somewhere against my will, somewhere dangerous, has an historical context I cannot ignore. Not in the face of the Orphan Bus. It seems like there has never been a time when I did not know how the Jews of Europe were loaded into cattle cars and transported to their deaths.

When I hold the two images of the Garbage Train and the Orphan Bus beside each other in my imagination, they blur into one long nightmare of a machine, a press of reeking flesh destined for the incinerator.

I have two newspaper articles side-by-side on my bulletin board. One is about the Anne Frank Exhibit that is touring the world, and local efforts to bring the exhibit to our University. The second is an article about a teenage beauty pageant held in Sarajevo after a year of siege. There's a photo of the event: Thirteen thin teens in high heels and

swimsuits are holding a banner that reads, "DON'T
LET THEM KILL US." The picture got out, but
they can't.

> Anne Frank no longer needs a photo. There's a
> popular portrait that's been reproduced so many
> times, it is there even when it's not; her face is
> stamped in my memory.

Isn't it inconceivable that there are young women
today who find themselves in situations as desperate
and hopeless as Anne Frank's? Inconceivable. I am
trying to inconceivable it away. But the articles are
right here. I could paper my walls with more of
them if I wanted. Stories about every kind of
injustice, in every part of the world. Stories of
pride in the face of humiliation, courage in the face
of death, and the flourishing of the creative spirit in
the face of complete oppression. Through the
legends of Anne Frank and Miss Teen Sarajevo we
are consoled by victories of the human heart.

> It's like the ancestors said, once one has seen the
> worst, somehow come through the worst, there is
> nothing more to fear. But is there no shame?

How can we relish these stories without some twinge
of shame at contributing to, or failing to prevent, the
conditions which demand such supreme
transcendence?

> I do not think we as humans should be taking so
> much pride in our invention and perfection of
> martyrdom.

I wonder what will happen to the babies from the Orphan Bus, and to the shrapnel-scarred adolescent beauties of Sarajevo. Their images haunt me, along with the eyes of Anne Frank. Surely she wishes we would put less energy into memorializing her and more into protecting the children who are here today. How frustrating for her to have been turned into an icon, to be part of the incessant labeling and categorizing that makes us incapable of saving each other.

> Or is it just frustrating for **me**? I have fallen into every trap. I have taken many bold stabs at the air, slashed artfully through empty space.

I would very much like to pin down a formula for the survival of humanity in this spirit-assigned manifesto.

> In the end, it is still just me and my sword. I touch the point to my chin: "Confess!"

Maybe saving oneself is enough — if enough of us make the effort. And if we are incapable of saving each other, maybe we shouldn't try. It is up to each of us to make ourselves fit to inhabit this earth. If we can each feel worthy of our planet, we might find a way to stop destroying it.

> I use my sword to draw a little circle around my feet and put myself on notice. At last the enemy has been engaged...

A Funny Thing Happened
On The Way To The Inquisition

or

I Thought I Knew What I Believed
But Now I'm Not So Sure

A Theater of the Mind
in One Act

Cast of Characters

INQUISITOR........Me
SUBJECT.......Myself
KIBITZER...........I

(The setting is an outdoor market or fair. A long table is draped with a white cloth. Behind it sits the INQUISITOR, a bearded man dressed in a white peasant blouse; he wears a bandana jauntily on his head and some mystical looking jewelry. On the table in front of him are three dice and a hand-lettered sign which reads, "Psychic." The SUBJECT is a nondescript thirty-something woman. She sits opposite the INQUISITOR, or tries to sit. She lacks muscular control, like a

44

sleep-walker, and flops off the chair from time to time; in between getting back into a sitting position, she answers the INQUISITOR's questions from a position of kneeling at and supporting herself against the table. The KIBITZER alternately hovers over the SUBJECT and circulates around the market at will, always remaining within ear-shot of what is going on at the "Psychic" table. As the scene opens, SUBJECT is trying to write her name, address, etc. on a pink piece of paper; she is writing in a spiral around some information already printed on the page, with great difficulty and much crossing-out, dropping of pen, crinkling of paper, and the like.)

INQUISITOR: *(unable to wait any longer for SUBJECT to complete her writing)* Roll the dice! *(He pushes the dice toward her.)*

SUBJECT: *(putting paper aside and rolling the dice)* There.

INQUISITOR: *(barely glancing at the dice)* As you know, we are here to find out what you believe.

SUBJECT: *(falling out of her chair)* I'm really not comfortable with the word, "believe," not since I heard someone say that believing something doesn't make it so.

INQUISITOR: And do you believe that?

SUBJECT: *(crawling back into the chair)* There it is again. What if I say yes? It's like saying, 'I always lie and that's the truth.' I believe that it's pointless to believe in anything.

KIBITZER: *(disgusted)* Evasive. Are you going to let her get away with that?

INQUISITOR: Do you believe that believing in something doesn't make it so, and why?

SUBJECT: You don't let up, do you?

INQUISITOR: We're here to confront the essential question: What do you believe? No use making it harder than it has to be.

SUBJECT: *(has fallen out of her chair again and is kneeling at the table)* But maybe it just doesn't matter what I believe; then this would all be a waste of time.

INQUISITOR: Do you really believe that? To whom wouldn't it matter?

KIBITZER: You're playing into her trap. Get on with it already!

SUBJECT: Can I roll the dice again?

INQUISITOR: I think that would be a good idea. *(SUBJECT rolls dice)* Good. Now, let's start at the beginning.

SUBJECT: I think I'm ready.

INQUISITOR: Once, you believed in God.

SUBJECT: Yes. When I was little I believed in God.

INQUISITOR: And...

SUBJECT: And everything. When I was little I believed everything I was taught.

INQUISITOR: In regard to...

SUBJECT: Everything! *(getting back into the chair)* OK, but in regard to religion mostly. That's what we're talking about, isn't it?

INQUISITOR: Is it?

KIBITZER: What is this, a therapy session? Ask the hard questions! Make her squirm!

INQUISITOR: When did you stop believing in God?

SUBJECT: *(struggling to stay in the chair, her eyes are riveted to the dice on the table)* That question implies I don't believe now.

INQUISITOR: It does not. *(he picks up the dice and hides them in his hand, causing SUBJECT to look into his face for the first time)* We are starting at the beginning and working forward. You said that as a child you believed in God, "and everything." When did you first stop believing?

SUBJECT: I consider the age of nine as my awakening, though it's probably just when all of the questions coalesced. I know that at nine I didn't feel God's presence, not in the way I thought one would if He was really there.

INQUISITOR: Oh?

SUBJECT: Well, I was a kid. I had been taking everything literally. I was told that God was all-knowing, all-seeing, all-powerful, the creator of the universe and the source of life. When it actually dawned on me what that meant, I could no longer anthropomorphize God. He didn't attend to my every action and thought, he didn't judge based on any scale a mere human could comprehend, and he wasn't even a "he" at all.

INQUISITOR: You stopped believing in Him.

SUBJECT: I didn't like the idea of something spying on me all the time, knowing all my thoughts, judging me. I figured if there was a God, a god God, not a man God, then It could not be angered or disappointed the way people can be. The only God I was prepared to believe in was one that at best gave only blessings and at worst was completely indifferent.

INQUISITOR: You were prepared to believe. And did you?

SUBJECT: Kind of. I guess I just didn't give it a lot of thought. What was the point?

INQUISITOR: What **was** the point? You didn't like the idea of God watching over you, but you weren't ready to completely give up on God either.

SUBJECT: I didn't like the idea of God judging me. But I wanted there to be something more.

INQUISITOR: Such as?

SUBJECT: Magic; power; energy; something beyond the rules and formulas and systems that delineate our perception of reality...

KIBITZER: You were just too lazy to study the sciences.

SUBJECT: Maybe so. It wears me out. *(she falls out of her chair)* I just remembered something! *(climbing back into chair)* I had this idea that everything I really needed to know, everything that was really **true**, was already known to me within my senses, within my bones. Does that sound dumb now?

INQUISITOR: Does it to you?

SUBJECT: No. I have a great deal more respect for scholarship than I used to, but my experience has generally supported my theory.

INQUISITOR: That's what you believe.

SUBJECT: Of course, believing in something doesn't make it so! *(she falls out of her chair)*

KIBITZER: Not this again!

INQUISITOR: When you were nine, did you or did you not believe in the rituals you continued to perform with your family?

SUBJECT: *(kneeling at table)* I did not.

INQUISITOR: None of them?

SUBJECT: I believed that everyone else believed in them; and somehow that was enough. I believed in the specialness, when it wasn't distorted by the anxiety of the preparations, and that there was a power or magic in the doing of something as prescribed and performed for so many generations. But I did not believe that God required these things.

KIBITZER: Almost right; but she's leaving something out.

INQUISITOR: Oh? What might you be leaving out?

SUBJECT: *(climbing back into her chair)* Yes! I am! I'm leaving out that the only thing I ever really believed, really wanted to believe, was that Elijah really did come and sip the wine from the *seder* cup.

INQUISITOR: Interesting. You believed in the spirit.

SUBJECT: Yes. I guess I've always believed in spirits, or been fascinated by them. I can understand a spirit.

INQUISITOR: You can?

SUBJECT: It has a connection to a life, a very specific life; yet, free of physical limitations, a spirit can be everywhere and access knowledge not readily available to the living.

INQUISITOR: You're excited about this.

SUBJECT: It explains a lot.

INQUISITOR: Like Elijah?

KIBITZER: And the Ouija board...

INQUISITOR: What's that?

SUBJECT: When we were teenagers we got into "psychic" stuff, Tarot cards, Ouija boards, putting each other into trances, that kind of thing.

INQUISITOR: You believed you were contacting spirits?

SUBJECT: I allowed for the possibility. But some of the spirits seemed nasty. It was less frightening to believe they just came from our imaginations.

KIBITZER: Just like with God, you only want to believe in something if it's going to be nice?

SUBJECT: Why would I want to believe in something evil?

INQUISITOR: Excuse me, but I'm asking the questions here.

KIBITZER: Mr. Bigshot!

INQUISITOR: What are your thoughts about evil?

SUBJECT: The evidence is all around us that humans are capable of selfish, malevolent and destructive acts. If we can conceive of doing good then we can conceive of doing evil, and the ability of the mind to filter and reinterpret information even allows us to do evil when we think we are doing good.

INQUISITOR: Who decides which is which?

SUBJECT: The individual, society, history... it's all a matter of perspective.

INQUISITOR: But not God's perspective?

SUBJECT: God is Good. What else are we worshiping when we worship God if not goodness? God is the ideal of good which we seek to embody within our individual selves. It's hard to believe in God and it's often hard to believe in the inherent goodness of humanity, yet we are desperate to do so...

INQUISITOR: Please return to the first person singular; you are not speaking for humanity here, but only for yourself.

SUBJECT: I believe that God is Good.

KIBITZER: A statement of faith!

INQUISITOR: And do you worship that Good.

SUBJECT: I honor it; I trust it.

KIBITZER: It's time now.

INQUISITOR: Your answers suggest that you are a fatalist.

SUBJECT: *(falling out of chair)* I rolled the dice, didn't I?

INQUISITOR: And what did that mean to you?

SUBJECT: *(getting back into chair)* The energies of the moment, the pull of gravity, my nervous system, the slope of the table, the texture of the tablecloth, your attitude... I rolled the dice and they came up a certain way and whether you told me anything about the configuration or not, and whether I believed you or not and whether you yourself believed or not, and whether I was dreaming or waking, a truth of the moment was revealed.

INQUISITOR: And that was good?

SUBJECT: It was good for me, was it good for you?

KIBITZER: Ha ha ha ha ha...

INQUISITOR: Very funny. Would you like to roll the dice again? *(he lines them up on the table)*

SUBJECT: Not right now.

INQUISITOR: Why?

SUBJECT: We're talking about them too much.

INQUISITOR: Oh. Are you superstitious?

KIBITZER: Is that like being a fatalist?

INQUISITOR: Let her decide.

SUBJECT: I'm tired. I want to stop.

KIBITZER: Baby!

INQUISITOR: We're not finished.

SUBJECT: And I don't think we ever will be. I don't have all the answers. I don't want to have all the answers. I like the mystery.

INQUISITOR: You like not even knowing your own heart?

SUBJECT: Who said I didn't know my own heart? *(looking accusingly at KIBITZER)* You?

KIBITZER: You're a very confused girl. Listen to yourself.

SUBJECT: When I listen to myself I am not confused. It's just the words that confuse everything.

INQUISITOR: Then let us return to being systematic. You were saying that as a teenager you became interested in the occult.

SUBJECT: Listen, I really am tired. How about if I tell you my theory of the spirits and we leave it at that?

INQUISITOR: You have a theory?

SUBJECT: Yes.

INQUISITOR: Not a belief?

SUBJECT: No comment.

KIBITZER: Now you've done it.

INQUISITOR: Please, proceed with your theory of the spirits.

SUBJECT: Very well. There is One spirit. It is what unites everything. It is embodied in matter and most noticeably in living matter. The spirit is integral to the development of consciousness and personality and it in turn becomes imbued with the characteristics of the beings it inhabits. When the organism dies, the piece of the spirit that was captured within it is released. For a time, it remains distinguishable from the One and continues to exist as "the spirit" of that particular individual, exerting cosmic energies in his or her behalf.

KIBITZER: Are you going to let her get away with "cosmic energies?"

INQUISITOR: For now. *(leaning forward)* Go on.

SUBJECT: But as time passes, these individual spirits are reabsorbed into the One.

INQUISITOR: Go on.

SUBJECT: That's it. That's my theory of the spirits.

INQUISITOR: How do you account for the persistent claims that ancient spirits, Elijah for instance, continue to be "channeled," or what have you, through modern consciousness.

SUBJECT: I suppose they could be re-invoked by collective memory. But like I said, I don't pretend to have all the answers.

KIBITZER: Are you going to let her get away with "collective memory?"

INQUISITOR: I thought you said you did have all the answers, that you had all the answers that mattered "in your bones." *(SUBJECT falls out of her chair)*

SUBJECT: But you see, that's an answer that doesn't matter.

KIBITZER: Oooohhhhh....

INQUISITOR: Then let's get back to fate.

SUBJECT: *(getting back into chair)* Doesn't matter.

INQUISITOR: No?

SUBJECT: It's a useful concept. It helps us accept things we have no control over, excuse the inexcusable, comprehend the inexplicable. And it has fractal qualities. You can apply it to the smallest personal incident and to the most historic epochal events. We have no basis for testing "fate" because the entire process can be said to be fated. I think it would be a lot harder to argue against fate than for it.

INQUISITOR: Certainly for one who believes in God; or shall we say, Good?

KIBITZER: Ah ha!

SUBJECT: It's like the dice. The rightness of the moment, the inevitability of the seemingly random event. You could call that Fate. But I don't want you to think that I would just surrender to any of these things: the spirits, God, fate. We haven't even touched on free will...

KIBITZER: No. And I'm still waiting to discuss "collective memory."

INQUISITOR: Actually, I think we are almost done here. You yourself volunteered the theory of the spirits. Now, I simply want to know, do you believe it?

SUBJECT: *(wearily)* Yes. For the sake of argument, I'll say yes.

KIBITZER: For the sake of argument?

SUBJECT: For the sake of ending the argument.

INQUISITOR: Good! And does your believing the theory of the spirits make it true?

SUBJECT: Can I roll the dice again?

INQUISITOR: If you must.

SUBJECT: *(rolls the dice and looks at them for a minute before exclaiming joyfully)* Yes!

INQUISITOR: Excellent!

KIBITZER: Wait! What about "cosmic energies?!" What about "collective memory?!" I think she's raised more questions than she's answered!

INQUISITOR: Silence! I am satisfied... for now.

*(The SUBJECT falls out of her chair and this time succumbs to sleep, flopping all the way to the floor to lie beside her chair. The KIBITZER shakes her but she does not wake. Leaving the INQUISITOR with a look of disgust, KIBITZER stalks out of the scene. The INQUISITOR carefully arranges the dice side by side so that the numbers facing up are **all one**. Curtain.)*

The Clothing Exchange

In my dreams, I am always trying on my sisters' clothes.
Perhaps I'm making more of this than is justified,
But I follow the progress of my dream self in these situations
With the anxious pride of a parent watching a toddler.
I would say I've reached the age of about four,
In dream years,
As I can now dress myself, with difficulty,
Right down to the shoes.

In my dreams, I am always trying on my sisters' clothes.
And these are indeed trying dreams.
Nothing fits.
Nothing "goes together."
Nothing adequately hides my flaws
While accentuating my merits.
My gyrations are exhausting.
The fabrics cling uncomfortably to my sweaty skin.
With every outfit, my body is obviously more imperfect.

In my dreams, I am always trying on my sisters' clothes
In the closets of the bedrooms of the house where we grew up,
The house we still return to.
Visits "home"
Are not complete without a rummage through
The bureaus in the upstairs bedrooms.
Our memories of adolescence

Mingle with Mom's mothballed woolens
In a carefully distilled collection of cast-offs.
Occasionally, an actual exchange is made...

In my dreams, I am always trying on my sisters' clothes.
It is important to note here that I am the middle daughter,
Which means that when our grandmother sewed two little outfits
To be shared among three little girls,
I first wore the smaller of the two and looked like my big sister,
And then I wore the bigger of the two
And looked like my little sister.
Now, when my sisters themselves show up in these dreams,
I cannot be sure that they really are themselves
And not just other versions of me.

In my dreams, I am always trying on my sisters' clothes.
This is in keeping with an old family tradition:
No woman of my clan ever goes to visit another
Without a few choice items that ...just might fit...
It's a form of matchmaking.
Recognizing the perfect something for the perfect someone
And then holding on to it for eight months or so
And *shlepping* it across the country in a nice shopping bag
So that it can assume its rightful place as
The most cherished garment in a whole wardrobe,
Is nothing less than a triumph.

In my dreams, I am always trying on my sisters' clothes.
Which reminds me of Aunt Alice,
The uncontested queen of the clothing exchange,
Mid-Atlantic division.
The back seat of her car is always piled high with
Hand-me-downs
From sisters and cousins and friends and nieces and
You-name-em.
She has a tendency to take in more than she gives away,

Which provides for a good selection.
Aunt Alice knows people and she knows clothes and
She doesn't like to see anything go to waste
Or anyone go without.
Is it any wonder that in my dreams everyone is grouped by size,
And we all share one closet?

In my dreams, I am always trying on my sisters' clothes.
And sometimes when I feel lonely I go to the thrift store
For a good browse.
No item costs more than five dollars,
Each has stood the test of time and laundering,
And everything is grouped and displayed with the perfect logic
Of normal, busy, practical women.
I have exchanged entire wardrobes of old old clothes
For new old clothes
At very little cost and with much pleasure,
Tho' not as much as if I'd had a sister or two along.

In my dreams, I am always trying on my sisters' clothes,
Searching for the perfect outfit.
But I can never get the right overall effect.
I put on a blouse, then have to change the pants to a skirt;
The skirt causes me to change from socks to stockings,
The stockings from sneakers to pumps,
The pumps need a jacket, the jacket needs a different blouse,
The blouse looks stupid with the skirt...
There are some mornings when I really **can't** get dressed;
Because I've gotten stuck in the dream.

In my dreams, I am always trying on my sisters' clothes,
Sometimes on the sly,
At risk of overstepping the bounds of sisterly generosity.
One way or another, I'm going to get caught
With my pants down.
Even my conscious mind chides my subconscious the next morning:

What are you doing back in those old places,
Looking at those old clothes?
You're your own person, you've got your own style;
Come on out of the closet now, girl!

In my dreams, I am always trying on my sisters' clothes.
Then I write down all of the details I can remember
In my journal:
The colors and styles and textures of the clothes,
What didn't fit and why, who was with me...
Something significant will surely be revealed.
Or does the obsessive need to be properly garbed only indicate
An unwillingness to be exposed?
Or am I simply heeding the ancient call
Of the clothing exchange?

In my dreams, I am always trying on my sisters' clothes;
And, lately, I also find myself perusing my friends' closets,
Even shopping,
Sliding hangers of new dresses along chrome bars.
I guess I'm ready to try on different identities, something new.
But I think I'll always have this nagging feeling
That there are a few garments that have worn so well,
So far,
That if I could only find them,
They would be just perfect for me.

The Dream

I have made some progress with
The Dream:
I have stalked it down the corridors of my childhood
And seen its shadow fall on the picture in the playroom;
And I have recognized this shadow as spirit vapor.
I have scoured the Dream Library and there
Turned the pages of a coloring book.
And, although the images blurred before my eyes,
The colors and shapes were familiar.
I have tried on dozens of outfits,
As if merely donning the correct costume
Might lift the curtain of this secret stage.
I have even visited the Museum Of Pain And Suffering,
And poked around in the nightmare section
Where the worst part is knowing that a lot of the terror
Is true.
I have gotten close enough to The Dream
To see it out of the corner of my eye
On more than one occasion.
In fact, near misses with The Dream
Are becoming almost frequent.
Yet here is where I always fail because,
Unfortunately, to touch The Dream
Does not give it more substance,
But only makes everything else less real.
I'm never sure exactly what I was doing in those moments,

Even an instant later,
And so have not been able to find a connection or clue.
It is absolutely possible that I have walked right through
The Dream
And later sensed nothing but a current of air at my back,
The slight click of a door closing behind me.
The entire process is becoming disconcerting.
I have been losing things lately,
And my memory is playing tricks on me.
It appears that in order to reconstruct this one image
I might have to disassemble my entire memory
Back to the beginning.
I'm not sure I'm willing to do this;
And I had this idea
While watching the sky the other night:
Look off to the side.
Some stars are so small and twinkly
You can't look directly at them.
You have to look off to the side.
Just so with dreams.

When I give up
Trying
To remember
The Dream,
It comes back to me on its own terms:

A shadow,
A shape,
A scent,
A season,
A sensation,
A whisper...
"...we're here..."

PART II

My Family's House

Visitations

My father's father came to the door of my dream;
He was wearing a hat and overcoat.
He may not have wanted me to recognize him.
He stood off to one side, in an empty space,
Apart from the dream, observing it.
I did recognize him,
And I went to him at once, leaving my dream behind.
He was stern, at first,
As any grandfather in ghostly form should be.
He reprimanded me for making a joke of death.
Perhaps the dreams he'd spied on had some perverse punchline
I didn't get.
I nodded obedience, if not comprehension;
And then I leaned over and kissed him on the cheek saying,
"I love you, Grandpa."

A dear old friend met me at a lounge in Boston.
She had left her wheelchair and all of her grey hairs behind.
She looked stunning, sitting at the bar,
Without a care in the world.
She too had something to tell me about death;
But I think it **was** a joke.
Then she walked me across the street,
To the building with the grand staircase
That splits in two at the landing.

I was left in the foyer,
Looking up at the polished wood.

My mother's father and his sister showed up unexpectedly.
They were dressed formally and walked arm in arm.
I saw them through the porch windows
Which I saw through the living room windows
As I made what seemed like my hundredth trip
Through the house.
This entrance was not supposed to be used,
But with much relief I found the doors unlocked.
They held themselves so tall and straight,
I had to stand on tip-toe to kiss their cheeks.
Instantly we were transported to the great hall
Where my entire family stood in a circle.
You see,
They seemed to say,
There's always another way.

Fine Linen

Everyone who is not absorbed in starting a family is obsessed with doing away with some kind of family bondage. Many do both, twisting new genetic rope into the future even as they unravel the strands from the past. It seems we must now purge ourselves of our childhoods, past lives, even ancestral memories. We can't explain it; we just feel all yucky inside. We bet that if we hadn't been yelled at as children we'd be less passive and more successful; or if we'd been breast-fed instead of bottle-fed we'd be more comfortable with our sexuality; or if we'd been allowed pets we'd know how to handle responsibility; or if we'd had rooms of our own instead of having to share with siblings...

I for one could not wait to re-invent myself as a separate entity from my family. I would make my own rituals, or none at all; think my own thoughts; draw my own conclusions; relate to the world as myself alone, not a representative of some specific race or gender. History, shmistory! (Oops, not so easy to re-invent, is it? Re-invent, shme-invent...) My family, bless them, I love them, I like them — but does that mean I have to be like them? Haven't we all at some time or another found ourselves in the middle of a family gathering asking: "How and when did these alien beings adopt me?" This must be where all of those stories come from of humans being suckled by wolves, or in some other way raised apart from society.

I grew up in the suburbs, in a split-level house. The public
schools I attended were homogeneously Caucasian and Christian.
If all of the "minority" students - Asian, Hispanic, Afro-
American, Jewish - were grouped together, we wouldn't have
made up more than two percent of all of those enrolled.
Dutifully, passionately, almost with a sense of urgency, my
parents undertook to instill the uniqueness of Jewish identity
within my sisters and me. We kept a kosher home, observed the
Jewish holidays, regularly attended synagogue and Hebrew
school, and were fully indoctrinated with the historic struggles
of our people. While our forebears had fought persecution and
intolerance so that we could attain the blessings of prosperity and
acceptance, our own enemy was assimilation. Several millennia
of cultural continuity could not be permitted to perish within the
smothering comforts of modern life. And so I learned to live
with a double identity.   Secular education alternated with
religious teachings, patriotism with Zionism. It was intended for
us to take the best of both, to preserve the past in the context of
the future, but the net result was that the present was terribly
confusing.

The closeness and richness of my family life was at once a
source of joy, pride, embarrassment and guilt. Everywhere I
turned were contradictions. In the context of the Christian
community, I was encouraged to stand up for my differentness,
but in the context of my Jewishness I was required to conform.
In a time of great social upheaval, when people of color
demanded equality, and youth protested the right of their elders
to send them to war, and women sought to break the patriarchal
reins that dictated their roles, and ecologists raised their voices
on behalf of Mother Earth, I was charged with maintaining an
identity of separateness while honoring the underlying likeness
of all creatures.

Even our own family history was riddled with
inconsistency. There were wide rifts between close relations
over degrees of religiosity, intermarriage, politics and money.
The historic narrative of recent generations was subject to

debate, revision and censorship, with emotions still running high over certain events and an unwillingness to dwell on the more brutal and depressing facts. My family wanted for us only to feel happy and free, yet our lessons were full of cautionary tales about how swiftly the outstretched hands of a friendly community could be replaced by the gauntlet of crushing oppression. Perhaps my questioning mind paid homage to a long tradition of scholarship, but it also served to deconstruct the faith it was meant to support. In direct proportion to the energy invested toward indoctrinating me with the "birthright" of Judaism, I was inclined to resist.

By the time I was fifteen I had begun to accept that life is often, maybe mostly, cruel. Further, I thought, whatever this thing called God is, it cannot save me from the pain of existence — what could prove this better than the history of the Jews? It even occurred to me that my existence would be a lot less painful if I could separate myself from the history of the Jews. Did I have to go through life on the defensive, alert to the slightest hint of antisemitism? Did I have to hate certain groups of people whose people had been the enemies of my people in the recent or distant past? Did I have to grieve for the losses and suffering of all the generations? Did I have to repent for the transgressions of my entire race? Did I have to perfect and continuously enact a repertoire of ritual in order to appease a watchful god? I had grown up with nothing but comfort and security, and yet supposedly I was involved in a fight for existence. I did not feel threatened by the enemies of my forebears. I felt more threatened by the forebears themselves. Their grief and anger would consume me. They would dictate every movement of my ritualized existence. They would extract from me the very breath of new life with which to make themselves immortal, and leave me the sour wheezing cough of decay. The big world was calling out to me, and there were times when I would fantasize about walking right out of the front door of that split-level house and walking away without ever looking back. I would walk away unburdened and commence to

discover myself in a long leisurely process, uninterrupted by
holy days, far from the judgmental gaze of a betrayed
community, deaf to the insistent demands of racial guardians.
But I did not have to run away. It was never meant for me to be
a prisoner; I knew that, somewhere in the depths of my teenage
heart. Soon enough I would go off to college with the full
blessings of my family, and there I would be free to decide for
myself to what extent I would follow the traditions of Judaism.

I suppose the irony of such an exquisitely ambivalent Jewish
youth as myself going to Israel on a summer holiday was not lost
on the zealous, overbearing American Zionist Youth Foundation
counselor who interviewed me prior to the trip. The six week
tour of Israel, with famed Israeli dance teacher, Fred Berk, was
a high school graduation gift from my parents. My love of folk
dancing made the excursion appealing despite my reluctance to
be further immersed in the Jewish milieu. I looked forward to
seeing a foreign land and to dancing every day. The AZYF
counselor obviously wanted me to express some deeper desire,
or conviction, or possibly just readiness, to grapple with Israel,
and he bullied me with impatient questions until I cried. I have
no memory of the actual words spoken, only of the feeling of
humiliation, as if some deep weakness had been revealed. I
disregarded the whole episode as soon as I received word of my
acceptance to the program. The interview had been a stalemate
after all. There was nothing really wrong with me. And he had
been out of line. He had no business probing into my personal
beliefs, testing my allegiances. But I still felt uncomfortable
about all of those tears, how I could have let his questions
devastate me. I went to Israel more determined than ever to
remain aloof from any specific relationship I might have with
that land. I would dance, I would sightsee, I would make
friends and take pictures and learn, but I would not be touched.
I would touch Israel, but it must not touch me.

I think everyone's sense of the import of American Jewish
youths going to Israel was overblown. Reading back over the

letters I sent to my family, it is clear that our experience of the adventure was pure survivalist. Much space is devoted to the physical travails of bus rides, strange food, outhouses, kibbutz farm work, and life with twenty-six other young women as my constant companions. By contrast, five days in Jerusalem is reduced to: "We saw the *Yad VaShem*, the Wailing Wall, the Holy Sepulchre, the model of Jerusalem at the Holy Land Motel, *Me'a Shearim* in Old Jerusalem, plus we had a bus tour around the Seven Hills and much much more — but we really didn't have much time to go exploring on our own or do any shopping." I can remember writing that letter and seeing those sights, the memories of which have stayed with me longer than those of the personal intrigues and physical challenges I recorded in such detail. It's good to know, now, that the magic of those places could penetrate my fog of ignorance, my supreme nonchalance. I remember standing at the Wailing Wall and willing myself to be unmoved. The tears came anyway, and they seeped out again at the Holocaust memorial. In other places I felt angry; in the bomb shelter of a kibbutz in the Golan Heights I was repulsed by the pride the residents showed in their survival tactics, the bright play area in a cement bunker. In the ruins of Mazada I sensed the ghosts of martyrs lingering penitently and wondered at the waste of their self-righteous suicides. And within the walls of *Me'a Shearim,* where the ancient bricks were recently graffitied with Zionist diatribes against Orthodox tradition, I made a bitter joke that there was more antisemitism in Israel than elsewhere in the world. Israel certainly didn't feel like my homeland. Everywhere, I was a stranger. We AZYF kids were oddities, humored, politely tolerated, and blanketly dismissed. Whatever our thoughts might have been about Judaism, Zionism, pacifism, sexism, you name it, they were pointed out to be of singular irrelevance to the realities of Israel and to flesh and blood Israelis. The dancing saved us from spontaneously combusting from the build-up of emotion. We danced our hearts out every day and slept the sleep of the dead each night.

I came home tanned, toned and surprisingly smug. I had come out of the land of the forebears unscathed, stronger if not more enlightened. Little lingering questions, such as why I cried at the Wailing Wall, were better left alone. With my departure to college I was officially turning my attention to other matters. More than anything I sought liberation of the mind, liberation from the necessity of every action and thought being filtered through a particular cultural and ideological lens. I gave up Judaism like you'd give up a bad habit. Cold turkey. The resulting identity crisis was uncomfortable, but uniquely mine. With some relief I recognized that it had nothing to do with Jewishness. How refreshing to finally change the subject after seventeen years.

Once free to establish my own life-style, and sufficiently distant from my hometown, my relationship with my family improved. The playing field was leveling. We had always loved and respected each other; now we no longer had to be embattled in a test of wills. I found I could be more tolerant of the rituals on my visits home, even gracious and mildly sentimental about them. That which I had so long resisted was comfortingly familiar. I also discovered a new appreciation for my upbringing. Too many of my fellow students appeared to be in emotional distress, lacked the discipline and direction to successfully manage their curricula, or allowed their energies to be consumed by hostile and self-destructive acts. That I should find myself a relatively confident and competent member of my freshman class, dubious and disoriented as I was, was a credit to the unconditional love and consistent integrity with which my parents raised me. That unyielding edifice of Jewish tradition was no longer a barrier against which I battered myself. It was a light tower, an anchor, something solid amidst a swirling, seething sea. Even when its shadow fell across my shiny new world, haunting me with the old refrains of worry, anger, grief and guilt, I was grateful for it. At least it was a place to start. Without antipathy I commenced the task of my personal re-invention. I wanted to give up hate, and that included self-hate. I wanted to be someone who was not defined by the past, who held no grudges, harbored no fears, carried no debts. I wanted to serve good by embodying it, not through blind obedience. I wanted simply to leave myself alone, nurture my creativity, and be in the world with an open mind and a loving heart.

I started to live my life according to my own rules — and was surprised that I had so many! Within five years of abandoning my kosher diet, I became a vegetarian. Within ten years, my regimen of vitamins and health foods was stringent, and essential to my sense of well-being. Instead of a Star of David, I wore a crystal around my neck and felt unlucky without it. I started my mornings with yoga instead of the *Shema Yisroel*. So much for leaving myself alone; I had succeeded only in replacing one set of rituals with another. And this idea of "being in the world" also proved misguided. I was far too analytical to just "be." I confronted, I interpreted, I judged; I pushed and pulled at every social structure that came under my scrutiny. And while it seemed impossible for me to "blend in," "sticking out" proved equally discomfiting. I observed in myself frequent feelings of intimidation, suspicions of unworthiness. I had spread my creative wings and dared myself to fly, but found that there was often no idea that stirred me. I was churning out my artwork from a sort of defensive posture, as if a sufficient quantity of product would justify my existence. Secretly, I was concerned that I really had nothing significant to say, that the work was pure self-indulgence.

By the time I was thirty, I just felt irritable. Control - or release from it - was not possible. I could neither change the current nor swim against it. The eddies carried me back into those deep, shadowy waters of Jewish identity with more and more frequency. I had failed to invent a new self in the face of an old world. I had failed to invent a self that felt fearless and free in place of one that felt afraid and vulnerable and angry. Where was my open mind? Where was my loving heart? How could I be in the "big world" if I forbade myself to be in my own little one? Years of resistance had weakened me, not made me stronger. If my artistic outpourings were missing the point, whose fault was that? I would never convey any universal truths if I refused to examine how they might be revealed through my own uniquely personal experience. It was time to go back to the beginning.

I began to explore my family history. My approach was simple: everything I had reviled and wanted to keep at a distance, I now embraced as a scholar. I turned my undivided attention to previously avoided aspects of my heritage, delving into embarrassing and painful matters with the zeal of a journalist. I made charts, studied maps, read history books and biographies, recorded interviews and studied Yiddish. I had no purpose, only process, and this was to get as much input as I could from a variety of sources and then to let that information strike what chords it may. This time around there would be no particular agenda. The filtering lens would be my own, the subject matter as broad or narrow as I chose.

My first challenge was to confront the emotional implications of descending from an historically persecuted people. It was time finally to admit that I had cried at the Wailing Wall just like everyone else there and for the same reason: I'm a Jew. My blood runs thick with ancestral memories of like-living, like-thinking, like-creating people. My old smell-brain recoils in fear, whimpers in pain, and laughs in pleasure via a genetic program that will take as many thousands of years to erase as it did to create. I trembled in grief at the Wailing Wall, a grief that was so much older and bigger than I was that I refused to accept it as mine. I found I could let myself touch that grief, once I recognized that the ancestors had not just dumped it on me; they were actually still around, helping to bear the weight. The forebears, it turned out, were on my side, neither hindrance nor threat. They were as invested in this process of self-discovery as I. And it was when I began to probe into the details of our family's experiences during the pogroms and the Holocaust that their spirits were revealed to me. They seemed to agree that these circumstances which drove my family from Russia and Poland had too long loomed like a black hole in our history. It had been as if we could neither go forward nor back. Ways of life, often life itself, ended. Those who lived then could not possibly have looked forward and seen us today. And we could not look back and find them, with so much historical record lost, and the fear of the black hole's despair. But my awareness of the spirits implied that the connection is never lost. I forced myself to go right up to the edge of the black hole and look down in it. I did not turn to stone, or salt. The black hole did not swallow me up. And when I raised my eyes I found that I did not perch at the ravelled edge of existence. What I saw was an entire bolt of fine woven linen unfurled across the contours of time. I could see across shocking tears and small imperfections to follow the ancestral line back and back in one continuous ribbon. "Despair not," the ancestral spirits whispered, "terror and tragedy are only the flaws in our fabric, not the stuff of it." At last I accepted the conditions in which my people had died, and I then found it possible to explore how they had lived.

As I began to research and document my ancestors' lives, I soon confronted a new dilemma. I needed a way to reconcile, or at least disregard, the inter-family conflicts that pitted one branch against another. I had no desire to take sides or in any way glorify petty details of personal animosities and affronts. There was nothing new in these stories, just more tragedies of intolerance, in miniature. And for the same reason I always felt uncomfortable identifying myself as a Jew - that aligning myself with any group at all supports divisiveness - I had no inclination to attempt a formal family biography. A point of view would inevitably emerge, a perspective dictated more by the availability of information than by the true significance of events. My mother and father, after all, are both of Eastern European Jewish stock; from my perspective their family stories are more similar than different. So I concluded that the usual delineation of maternal and paternal lines was insignificant to my personal inquiry with the ancestors. The historical connections between the characters in my family album were not as necessary to document as the psychic connections between them and their times, between their times and my times, and between them and me. In me, all elements combine; it matters very little now through what exact routes they passed down.

Still, my findings did demand some order; certain generalizations could be made. A friend gave me the key. She told me that as a child she believed that women gave birth to women and men gave birth to men. This was because when she read the Bible in her youth, she noticed that all of the "begats" referred to male names, and deduced that if these fathers had only these sons, then all daughters must come from only mothers. We had a good laugh over this, but later I thought how much truth there was to it. For all that I am mostly my mother's daughter, that part of myself which relates to maleness is mostly my father's son. I recognized that an appropriate division of my family history would be by gender, since here is where the experiences of past generations diverge within a common culture. My "maternal line" would refer to **all** of the women on my charts, and my "paternal line" to **all** of the men. Having thus organized my chorus of ancestral voices, I began to examine the family narrative as a means of both framing and answering some of my personal questions. I got more than I bargained for, and not exactly what I expected.

I had leapt into my family research with the stoic determination of a warrior. I would confront all of my demons and cast them out. I would open the festering sores and cleanse them, no matter how painful. If I had acted shamefully, I would repent; if I had been shamed I would retaliate. But I did not find myself on a battlefield. The demons I encountered turned out to be parts of me; it was possible to befriend them. And the ancestral spirits forbade despair. There was no judgment and no penance. Having seemingly snubbed every tradition my people held dear, I was nonetheless ushered into their sacred space. "It's the questions that bind us together, not the answers," the voices murmured. "It's the lust for life; it's the prayer for peace." I began to recognize the great portico, the long hallways and the twisting stairways of my dreams.

This is my family's house. Memories from all the ages circulate through well-worn rooms in which every detail of furnishing and fixture tells a story which tells a story which tells a story, down to the very foundations, which spring from the oldest and longest story of all, the Earth. Here in my family's house, there are places to rest in the stillness of the past, and familiar voices speak comfortingly, sometimes drawing back a curtain to reveal a beautiful landscape. Here in my family's house, I find that the big and little troubles of my people no longer embarrass me. I tell our stories with pride and embellish them with pleasure. Each iteration teaches me something about how not to feel afraid, angry and embattled. Here in my family's house, I discover the elements of my composition. All that existed before me resides here, available for my exploration, and these elements do not in themselves ever change, regardless of my level of attention and comprehension. I will re-invent myself again and again, but always out of the same materials. Here in my family's house, I must acknowledge that wherever I might be going, this will always be where I come from. Some might call this bondage, but I call it fine linen.

Sacred Space

Sharp Tongued Women

I come from a line of sharp tongued women. They did not really live in the faded, silent, monochrome world of those old photographs. Life was not all frozen solemnity but quite the contrary. Behind the placid group portraits there must have lurked immense tension — what with the closeness of all those cousins.

They would have had bustling homes on bustling streets filled with pungent smells and laughing children. And the feelings run deep and close to the surface at once: Love, pride, faith, devotion, envy, weariness, frustration, fear, hunger...

When there is food, there is never a shortage of mouths to feed and we work like slaves in the kitchen, making the children help and feeding them a little because the men always pray at table - at our beautiful table full of steaming plates - until the meal is nearly cold. This is to show God that we willingly sacrifice the comforts of our flesh for the goodness of our souls. We say: Show thanks for the food by eating and enjoying already. We were not put here to starve; we have work to do and we need strength to do it. When you join the angels you can pray all day.

I come from a line of sharp tongued women — sharp of tongue and soft of shape. They taunted their men with those sharp tongues to show them that they too could be witty and wise. And they ate all they wanted, when the table was full, so as to tempt with round womanly folds, and to give thanks for life simply by living it...

   After all, we are daughters of Sarah, Mother of Nations. The vessels and bearers of faith and race, we are blessed in our natural state. No flesh must we sacrifice. God might require of Abraham the blood of the ram or the foreskin of the son, but before Mothers of Nations, who have bled and birthed and bled with moon and tide and season, God is humbled by Its own perfection. We keep the Holy Days and Festivals in our homes because we are keepers of the Moon. Men and God attempt to know one another through negotiations and examinations. Mothers of Nations participate in the perfection of existence and experience the wholeness of God's work. This is our prayer.

   I come from a line of sharp tongued, indomitable women, and pious, disciplined, dominating men. In the house of many rooms where my dreams take place, I hear their voices raised in cheerful gossip, or murmuring their prayers, or in bursts of half-suppressed quarreling or love-making. From room to room I look for them. Waking, I find I am them.

Women's Work — Men's Work

KNOCK KNOCK
KNOCK KNOCK KNOCK
Now why doesn't she answer? I know she is always home making pumpernickel bread on Thursday.
KNOCK KNOCK KNOCK
"Tova! Tova! Are you there? It's me, Dottie."
KNOCK KNOCK
She is not answering on purpose. She hopes I will go away. But I will not. I will not! Even though my arm is falling off and my feet are chopped liver, I will make her answer. If she does not come to the door in one minute, I will go to the side and tap on her window.
KNOCK KNOCK KNOCK
"Tova!"

"Dottie? Is that you? You are so good to wait for me. I was right in the middle of making the loaves, you know how I always make bread on Thursdays."
Since when does it take her so long to make a pumpernickel? She always brags about how nimble she is. And her hands are scrubbed clean, and I can smell baked bread already. *Oy!* What a story! "Tova, Tova, who would dream of spoiling your loaves? But I come like always on Thursdays with milk for you. Don't you want any this week?"
"The milk! Of course! Oh, Dottie, here I've kept you waiting and you've been *shlepping* that milk pail around all

morning. Now put that heavy thing down there on the step for
a minute and I'll bring my jar out."

Still she doesn't invite me in. To think it comes to this
between friends!

"Here we go! No, let me pour, Dottie. Your arm shakes,
it's so tired. There! Now your load is lighter. And here is
what I owe you."

If she thinks I'm so tired I will not press her for the other,
she doesn't know me. "Yes, we are all caught up on the milk.
But Dov specifically asked me to collect for Yehuda's lessons,
too."

"Yehuda's lessons? You mean to say Mortcha has not paid
for the lessons? Since when?"

"Since when do I see your Mortcha for him to pay me?
The lessons have not been paid since four Thursdays ago when
you last paid me!"

"But I told Mortcha to give the money to Dov after they
study with the *Rebbe* on Sundays."

"You know my husband takes no money directly. His
service is to God; the proper Judaic education of our young men
is a *mitzvah*. It should be free. Who can put a price on such
work? What pious man would dare to? It should be free. Like
the seven children he gave to me. Free. For nothing he gave
them to me. For love. Not a penny more. A wonderful gift.
And wonderful children. But free they are not. They cost,
Tova, you know this. They cost and cost. There are shoes,
shirts, school books... But let us not begrudge all of our toil and
hardship to feed and educate them. They are an investment.
Your Yehuda is a smart boy. He will be a great man and take
care of you some day. And he will take a good Jewish wife and
raise many fine children and conduct all of his business
according to the laws of the Torah, which will bring great
naches upon the entire family. And for this he will have my
Dov to thank. How will he feel knowing that his good fortune
comes at the expense of another?"

"Now, Dottie, you have gone too far! To suggest that we

would steal our son's lessons! You insult us! Your husband is a trusting man, and devoted to his work. He teaches without concern for petty debts and schedules. In this he is a fine example to all of us; he is his own best example of faith and duty."

"Well, of course, my whole family then is a fine example of how the spirit alone can nourish; you could come to my house and hear for yourself. Only sometimes our stomachs complain so loudly that I worry God will not be able to hear our prayers."

"Shame on you, Dottie! I'm glad Dov can't hear you speak like this. We have no desire to see your family suffer, especially not over such a simple misunderstanding. Let me see what I have in the house. If it is not enough, I will have the rest for you next Thursday."

Still she won't invite me in. Now it is because she pities me. She doesn't want me to see what she has and I do not. How I hate pity! Yet it is my special talent to make people pity me. Is it my fault that this is the only way I can get them to pay? Is it Dov's piety that prevents him from asking for money, or his pride? Well, he had better have enough pride for the both of us — and I, God willing, will collect enough pity to feed all nine of us! Ah, here she comes.

"Just as I thought, that milk money is the last I had in the house. But here, take this pumpernickel and this jar of chicken *shmaltz* as a sign of my good faith. I will talk to Mortcha and we will work it all out when I see you next week. Oh, and if you should make some cheese this week - I see you have quite a bit of milk left - bring some along for me. Your milk and cheese are the best, you know. God **does** hear your prayers, Dottie. He smiles on your home; even your cows are blessed."

She is a good friend, Tova. So what if this bread is already baked and cooled when she claimed to be in the middle of kneading it not ten minutes ago. "You're too generous, Tova. You shouldn't have - but since you offered - I can't resist such a **fresh** loaf..." She still has dimples when she smiles, my Tova. We played many games together as children, even this one, where we'd imitate our mothers haggling with each other. It's a serious game now, but still a game. "Until next week, then, Tova. Good health. My best to Mortcha and Yehuda."

"My best to your family, Dottie. But one more minute. Come close; I have something to say to you."

Now what? "Yes, Tova?"

"Does he treat you well? Is he kind to you? You look terrible. You are doing too much. I don't know how you keep going."

"Dov is a good husband, Tova. A good father. I should be such a good wife and mother as he is a husband and father. There is men's work and women's work, Tova. You know this is how it is. We didn't make it this way, but we live with it. *Nu?* I don't look so good? Well, don't worry. It isn't because my Dov is keeping me up all night. I have a little blessing for every day of the week already!"

"Dottie! You're terrible!"

"And if next week you would invite me in, I will say even more terrible things — just because I like to see your dimples. *Sholem*, Tova."

"*Sholem*, Dottie."

My Dream Hair

Dream Journal Entry

I dreamt I had very long, beautiful hair and was very proud of it.

What Hair We Had

What hair we had
Thick long ringlets all a'tangle
Blondish red
Turning to reddish brown as we grew older
When the curls would loosen and fall like waves
Below our slender young shoulder blades
How we'd brush and brush those tendrils
Every day a hundred strokes
If our dresses were threadbare
No one noticed
They only saw our lustrous locks
Our gleaming rosy round faces
Sheyna meydelach we were
Allowed this one vanity of the hair
Just long enough to capture
That single worthy heart
For whom we'd then forsake our flaunting femininity
Don the *sheytl*
Lower the lashes
And commence the duties of the wife
To be admired for our orderly households
Our well-mannered children
The bounty of our table
But never again for the sensuousness
Of that glistening cape of hair

Even the most enthusiastic of scholars
Has been known to sometimes rest his book upon the table
And his arms upon his book
And his head upon his arms
And close for just a moment his weary eyes
How wicked it would be, just then
For the dreams of this pious servant of God
To be infiltrated by waterfalls of hair
A woman bending over him
Her silken curls brushing his hand
And, heaven forbid, it might be a married woman
The wife of a friend, a business partner
Heaven forbid and so man forbids too
Forbids himself temptation, and we our tresses

What hair we had as girls
As married women we lop it off and hide it
But under the *sheytl* and the *tichel*
It keeps growing back
Are we to blame if these miscreant curls
Will sometimes tickle the nose of an old Rabbi
Dozing over his prayerbook?

Hair

The Wig Makers

All of the sisters had lovely hair. But Hanaleh's was the longest and thickest and straightest. Every day when she would walk by the *sheytl* maker's shop the *sheytl* maker would come to the door and speak to Hanaleh:

"Tell your mother I will pay her by the pound for your hair! What a waste for a little girl to have such hair! It will grow long again twice or thrice before you are of marriageable age. And anyway, your papa has made a match for you already. Tell your mama I will pay her a full head's worth for only what grows below your shoulders."

To which Hanaleh would reply, "Mama says a nice girl should not sell her hair unless she is starving to death. And she does not want people thinking we are starving. Papa says the boy's parents will break the engagement if I sell my hair, but I don't like that boy anyway. So I don't want to ruin my hair either; I want to have my pick of all the boys."

"Ruin your hair? Since when does a haircut ruin one's hair, or one's reputation? Such a lot of nonsense. If you are so proud of all that hair, you had best keep away from the boys. As soon as one marries you, you'll be bringing that plait to me in exchange for a *sheytl*!"

The words of the *sheytl* maker troubled Hanaleh. She observed her mother and her aunts, the married women she knew. At home they all wore the *tichel*, a scarf over the head. Some wore the *tichel* when going out also, pulling it forward on the forehead to cover every inch of hair. The others would put on the *sheytl* to go to the market or *Shul*, a wig of human hair but still a wig, lacquered into an old fashioned bun and often ill-matched to the wearer's complexion. One day Hanaleh's mother noticed her daughter watching worriedly as she pulled the *sheytl* over her head, pushing stray wisps of her own hair under the silken net of the wig. She was wearing her *Shabbes* dress and pearls. "It is like going in two directions at once, is it not, Hanaleh? We put on our finest clothes and fuss over our appearance and then tie up our pretty hair in a rumpled wig just to be **not** so beautiful."

Hanaleh observed her sisters and cousins as they grew older and married. They all bought *sheytls* right away, and swore they'd keep the long locks that their amorous young husbands had praised so highly. But by the time their first child was born, usually within the year, the impracticality of this compromise had become obvious. The *sheytl* was even more uncomfortable and ill-fitting over a pile of long hair. And the hair itself grew limp and dull, as if mourning its confinement. If the rigors of pregnancy did not break the new brides' resolve, the sticky grabbing hands of their infants did. One by one they made their visit to the *sheytl* maker.

Hanaleh observed that while all of this hair-hiding was going on among her female family members, their male counterparts - blessed with the same vigorous follicles - sported their hair unashamedly. They grew long beards and side curls and bushy mustaches. Even their eyebrows seemed especially thick and prominent. Their names were Berish for Bear and Aryeh for Lion in celebration of their manly hirsuteness. Finally, Hanaleh noticed that when her male cousins married, they walked with their heads held high and their shoulders thrown back, with long assured strides. They no longer shuffled down the street, fearful schoolboys trying to look preoccupied by their studies while covertly eyeing young women's wrists, waists and waves. What a contrast to their wives, who had once sauntered down the street in hip-swinging, loud-laughing packs, but now scurried about with eyes always lowered and a long list of chores and duties awaiting their attention.

Hanaleh knew that the home was Mama's castle as well as Papa's, that in the house Mother held her head up and commanded great respect. But the words of the *sheytl* maker haunted Hanaleh. Now she had many admirers, but soon the sparkle of her eyes and the lustre of her hair would be reserved for one man only. "Then it had better be a deserving man," Hanaleh thought, "and not that pasty-faced *klutz* they've engaged me to. So what if his father is so learned and his mother's family is rich, I will not have him."

Expecting the worst of reactions to her decision to break the engagement, Hanaleh went to see the *sheytl* maker. "I will give you the bottom length of my hair, from the shoulders down, if you will teach me to make wigs and give me a job in your shop."

"Consider it done! If you have nimble fingers, we will both get rich. There is more business than I can keep up with, and plenty of beautiful hair to work with still — I will not even take yours until we run low. There, how is that for an agreeable arrangement?"

It was very agreeable. At least Hanaleh did not have to further enrage her father by appearing with a cropped head on the same evening she would proclaim her intentions not to accept his choice of a son-in-law. And with acceptable employment at hand, there was little her father could threaten.

A sensible man, Hanaleh's father chose not to disown a daughter who would soon be contributing her own income to the household. And the household would need her help. The no-longer-parents-in-law-to-be would have to be bought off somehow, with many gifts. It would cost about as much as a wedding, with no son-in-law to show for the expense. All of this went through his mind as Hanaleh stood stubbornly before him. He looked at her for a long time. He knew her to be strong physically, not just strong-willed, good with the hands, and sensible, a sharp girl.

"If you would rather go to work for *gelt* than for a husband, so be it. Besides, that *klutz* would be no match for you. His parents will thank me someday for saving him from my *meshugenah* daughter." A sensible man, Hanaleh's father was also a happy man as she thanked him with the utmost in humble respect and then ran shouting and laughing to tell her anxious sisters and mother.

The *sheytl* maker had been right about the potential of her business. Working together, she and Hanaleh became prosperous. Hanaleh sometimes traveled to neighboring towns to collect orders and deliver the finished *sheytls*. On one such errand, Hanaleh met the man she would marry.

"He is the one," she told her old friend. "For his smile to shine upon me day in and day out, I would forgo the attentions of all other men."

"So, I will get that full head of hair at last; it's grown in nicely, hasn't it, since we completed our bargain?"

"Yes, it has; and no, you won't. I'll wear the *sheytl* **over** my hair."

"Oh, they all say the same thing; you know that! Now tell me, what will your father say to having to make a wedding for you after all you've put him through? And this fellow is the son of saloon keepers!"

"There'll be nothing to say. I'll make my own wedding. I can afford it. After all, **I'm** a *sheytl* maker!

Critical Points

Summer, 1918 — Serock, Poland

I understand I have been near death with the influenza. Everyone has finally stopped weeping and praying over me, and trying to force chicken soup down my gullet. Now I am left alone to rest and try to reconstruct the fortnight that has gone by since I first took to this bed.

I remember the morning that I woke up with my limbs feeling so heavy and numb I could barely swing my legs over the side of the bed. My head, which had ached just a little the night before, thundered with pain. I must have rolled back under the sheets. I am quite certain that was on two Mondays ago.

I woke again, this time to the commotion of the three sisters who share my room moving out all of their belongings and bedding. I think this was under the supervision of Doctor Minzer and Father. It was terribly hot.

Mother sat in the corner of the room and prayed and wept continuously. Aunts and uncles and neighbors came and went but were not permitted past the threshold. They stood at the door with my siblings and peeked in sadly. Whenever I opened my eyes, someone was there to speak to me. Father and Aunt Chaya were the ones who tended to me, and to Mother, who was literally sick with worry.

I suppose four days and nights went by like this. Because the next time the doctor visited I heard him tell Father that he would have to break the Sabbath to heat water for my

compresses and soups and teas. I distinctly remember Doctor
Minzer saying that the next twenty-four hours would be critical;
if I could live through them, I would recover. I felt almost as
if I had died already. I no longer felt connected to the body
everyone was worrying over; my feverish dreams kept distorting
what I thought to be reality. But when I heard what the doctor
said, I made a decision that if my dear mother and father were
going to break the Sabbath to care for me, I would have to live.
I wished so much I could have spoken so I could have said this
to Mother to ease her fear.

"I'm going to the cemetery to pray over my mother's
grave." I remember how Mother said this and how Father and
Doctor Minzer began shouting at her that she was not strong and
would make herself sick as well. I felt irritated by this scene,
since I knew I would live no matter what. I wondered what
Mother thought *Bobe* Leah could do for me and why it was
important for her to be at the graveside. Wasn't my grandmother's spirit everywhere? I guessed that Mother just didn't
feel comfortable sitting in the house watching the Sabbath being
broken...

"That's right. That's exactly right. I'd rather sit here with
the headstones. It is a purer place to pray than a house in which
there is no *Shabbes*." It was Mother. She was sitting beside me
but we were no longer in my bedroom. We were in the
cemetery and I was lying atop *Bobe* Leah's grave. The fresh air
was lovely. It was dusk. The Sabbath Queen stepped right out
of the sky wearing pink robes and a golden crown. As she
walked toward us the sky behind her darkened but she continued
to glow pink and gold. She came up to Mother and placed a
gold crown like her own on Mother's head, and all the while
Mother prayed and pleaded with *Bobe* to carry her prayers to
God. Then the Sabbath Queen placed a black cloak over top of
me so that I could no longer see and no longer hear.

This was the only time I was really afraid during this entire
ordeal, when I was lying in the cemetery with the cloak of night
blotting out all of my senses. In fact, I became terrified that I

would not be able to keep my promise to live. I was choking, suffocating. My father was breaking the Sabbath and my mother was making herself crazy and all for nothing. I would die anyway. The next breath I took was so painful, with that cloak weighing down on my chest and face, that I thought it would be my last.

But, just then, the cloak was lifted away. It was lifted away by my grandmother! And it was not the cloak of night at all, but just the big quilts that had been piled on top of me in my sick bed. *Bobe* lifted away the blankets and oh, so kindly, just like I remember, touched my forehead and my cheek with her cool hand. Then, before she left, she tucked something under my pillow and whispered in my ear, "Not yet, child."

Sabbath morning, ten men came to the house and prayed. I was well enough to feel horrible. I can remember wishing they would leave. My tongue felt so thick it almost choked me and my throat felt like fire. I had no voice at all. With the greatest effort I could barely shift my legs or raise my arms. But when Father saw me watching him as he brought in another steaming kettle of water to set near the bed, he almost somersaulted with delight. The short service was about to end and he rushed to the front room to add his voice to the final prayer. Someone was sent to bring Mother home. I drifted off to sleep wondering if she would still be wearing her crown...

I don't think I woke again until Sunday because the next thing I heard was my brothers reciting their lessons under the tree in the back yard. Still I had no voice. I opened my eyes to find Mother sitting beside me just as she had in the cemetery. That's when I remembered about *Bobe* Leah's gift. I lifted my hand up to my pillow and tried to find the packet she had left there for me.

"Welcome back," Mother said, and then she took my hand in hers and patted it. "You saw her, didn't you?" I nodded. "And she left something for you, under the pillow?" I nodded again. Mother gently raised my head with one hand and felt all the way under the pillow with the other.

"I don't find anything under the pillow now," she said, helping me settle back more comfortably. "But I do not doubt you were given a great gift; we were all given a wonderful gift. Do you know what it is?" I could do nothing but look at her with wide eyes. "Your life. Cherish it, my daughter."

Fall, 1954 — Atlanta, Georgia

This has been the worst year of my life, the year I got old. I am going into the hospital for my third surgery on this stupid body that has turned into a falling-apart house. Every system needs to be fixed. I suppose I should stop being angry about it and be grateful for what the doctors are able to do these days. But I am angry. I have taken very good care of myself. Also, I have the good fortune to live in a country where the government and my neighbors are not trying to kill me. After everything my family has suffered, after all of the sacrifices they made for me, after all of their senseless premature deaths, how dare I falter like this. We will never get on our feet again; think of all of the medical bills. Perhaps I will never get on my feet again at all. I will be an invalid. Who will take care of me? My husband is working himself to exhaustion as it is. My children have their own lives. Why am I being punished? Other people do not try nearly as hard as I to observe the laws and traditions, yet they are robust and carefree. I do not begrudge them their happy healthy lives, but why am I not among them?

When I say my prayers tonight I will not pray for myself, but for my dear mother, may she rest in peace. She always felt for everyone else more than for herself. I will leave it for God to decide. If Mother needs me with her, God must send my spirit to where hers resides. But if Mother needs me to finish my work here, God must make me healthy. I feel foolish writing like this. No matter what I feel or do or pray or write, the Book of Life has already been written. I believe what my mother believed and hers before her: that whatever is to be has already been decided. We do not pray for God to re-write the Book, but only to ensure that what is written is carried through. God is very busy; I do not think it is a sin to send a friendly reminder from time to time. If it were, prayer would be forbidden.

I have had the surgery and I think I will live and be well again, now that Mother has visited me. While I was in the recovery room, I saw Mother come to my bed. She soothed my forehead with her cool hand. She didn't speak except to say "There, there," several times. Funny, when I woke up I thought at first that I was a teenager again, waking up from being so sick with the flu. I thought I heard Mother's voice saying, "Cherish your life, daughter." And I reached to feel under my pillow but found nothing there. Then I touched my hair, and felt it to be cut short, its coarseness a reminder of how grey it is. Suddenly, this no longer disappoints me, that those soft reddish locks are so long gone. Suddenly, I feel very thankful for this old grey head.

Winter, 1992 — Wilmington, Delaware

Every single time I wake up, I am certain that the woman sitting in the chair in the corner of my room is my mother. But usually it is my daughter and sometimes it is one of my granddaughters. I don't want to see anyone else. I mean, I don't want anyone else to see me. I'm sure I look terrible. This is not the way I want to be remembered, a woman on her deathbed.

How can I have grown so old and not prepared myself for this? Once or twice before I had prepared myself for death but death was not ready for me. Now I know I have come to the very last page of the very last chapter of my life, but I am unwilling to turn it. A long and often painful story, but never boring; I hate for it to end.

I wish they would understand that I can see anyone I want now. These deathbed visits are really unnecessary. I have been transporting myself to the homes of each of my loved ones. I visit their dreams; I stand in their kitchens and watch them cook and eat and talk and laugh. I can make my own farewells. And I can't visit with people here in my room as they would like, because this place is filling up with spirits and it is terribly distracting. Hundreds of voices are whispering to me night and day. They have waited a long time for me to join them; now they are here to help me find the way...

I woke up and felt that something had been laid on the bed next to my right hand. I began patting the covers, looking for it. "What is it you're looking for? Can I help?" It was my granddaughter, the middle one, the one I told all of my stories to, and she was looking at me like she knew.

"Nothing, it's all right," I said, and tried to make my hand be still.

She looked a little disappointed but didn't ask again. I remember being curious like that. I remember suspecting that below the surface of our daily routines and habits, marvelous, magical events transpired. How else could my mother and aunts transform the drudgery of housework into joyous ritual? And I found I could do the same. Now that I have this strange power, I like to surprise my friends in mundane moments. When I find them washing dishes or cleaning the stove, I breathe like a tickly feather in their ear or make the sound of their names being called from far away. It's to remind them, the Spirit is everywhere...

That granddaughter caught me talking to no one again. She was very tactful about it. Now I am certain she knows what is going on, but I do not feel able to discuss it. When she sits in the room with me she too appears to be listening to the voices. Good, in that case she will be able to make this last entry for me. She will know to write that in the end, waking became the dream and sleeping became the waking; and that when I woke for the last time, I did find a packet under my pillow, and I took it in my hand, and rose from the bed and went to my mother's side.

Mother and *Bobe* Leah may rest at last, for I have become the keeper of the secret gift. It is my turn now to protect and bestow the blessing of the matriarchs whenever our descendents call out in need.

The Seventh Sister

Sometimes the charts and the narrative just don't match up:

Mooska had seven daughters...

>Rita
>Ida
>Sylvie
>Mamie
>Ruth and
>Mini.

That's only six.

>Well, there was Mooska herself and
>Leiba
>Tzippa
>Rikfa
>Leah
>Fega and
>Pesah.
>That's seven.

No, now you're talking about Mooska's **sisters**!

What was the question?

Mooska's **daughters**. There were seven, but I only have six names: Rita, Ida, Sylvie, Mamie, Ruth and Mini.

Mini wasn't Mooska's daughter.

But that's what you just said.

I was mixed up. Mini is one of Leiba's daughters. Let's see. Leiba had five daughters:
Devora
Rifka
Latke
Mini and
Rose

I thought Rifka was a sister of Leiba and Mooska.

This was the niece Rifka. They were both named for the mother's sister, Rifka Chava.

Mooska's mother's sister?

Who else? You see, Mooska was the seventh sister.

Yes, she was a seventh sister. But she herself had seven **daughters**. If I take Mini out, I only have the names of five of Mooska's daughters now: Rita, Ida, Sylvie, Mamie and Ruth.

Well, I know the sixth one. That would have been Tamara.

Rita, Ida, Sylvie, Mamie, Ruth and Tamara. And...?

Those were Mooska's daughters.

Are you sure she had seven? You keep only naming six.

> Oh, she had seven daughters all right. Everyone knows
> there were seven Kaslevich sisters. But only the six
> came to America:
> Rita
> Ida
> Sylvie
> Mamie
> Ruth and
> Tamara.
> I'm not sure what happened to the seventh.

I see. And you don't even know her name?

> I'm an old lady. It's a miracle I can get even this
> much straight.

(It's a miracle you could forget the seventh sister.)

> What's that?

Nothing. I'm just going to leave a blank here for the
seventh sister. If you think of her name, let me know.

> You want to dig up all the family secrets, don't you?

Oh, is there some secret about the seventh sister?

> Mooska? Heaven's no. There's nothing secret about
> Mooska...

The First To Come

We ran barefoot all summer, my sisters and I, and never thought it a hardship, although the truth was, our parents could not afford to buy shoes for us. The aunts and uncles who were better off passed down pairs of shoes from their children, but by the time these reached us they were quite worn out, having carried so many feet already. In winter, we would each have a pair of short boots, new if there was nothing suitable from the cousins or an older sister. I think a collection was taken among the family, for winter boots and other necessities that my parents could not provide. This was appropriate as my father was the scholar of the family; he had no skill but teaching and for this he never pressed for compensation. It was right for his brothers and sister to help him.

Certainly it would have been preferred for my father to have married a woman of means whose parents would have helped set him up in business. Instead, he was hastily married to his first cousin, the eldest of five daughters, in order to make way for the marriage of the second daughter, for whom an offer had been made by a wealthy older man. My mother's dowry was two cows and a clutch of hens, which became the principal source of income for our household. This is how matchmaking often went in our city, especially for those with many daughters: a poor match had to be made to create an opportunity for a rich match, or matches were made between cousins as a way to keep modest savings within the family and because outsiders demanded larger dowries. My father's sister, who was as observant as he but

105

with a great deal more vigor, had married well to a tradesman
and had four sons, which she considered a splendid opportunity
to help out her nieces.

In my barefoot youth, of course, I was innocent to all of
this. I only knew that it was like a holiday to spend a week with
my Aunt Rifka and Uncle Temme in their little town twenty
miles from Vitebsk. I was treated like a daughter. And with the
boys always at market helping their father, or away to religious
studies and apprenticeships, there was peace in the big house and
it was my pleasure to help Aunt Rifka with her chores.

My own home was full of hens and bickering, with Father
bellowing for quiet and Mother exhausted but stoic. My eldest
sister ran the house, while Mother sold the milk and eggs. This
sister, already too old to expect a good match, became bitter and
mean. She hated to see an idle hand. My duty was the endless
mending of all of our clothes. When I could sit no longer nor
stand the glares from my older sisters who cooked and swept and
sweated far in excess of the demands of the minuscule hovel we
called home, I would go to the market and see if I could find
things that had dropped out of carts and baskets so I might try to
sell them again. Also, I would spend much time studying the
shirts and embroidered linens on display in the stalls so that later
I could practice sewing fancier things than patches.

It was a great honor when I was permitted to help with the
sewing for the wedding of one of Aunt Rifka's sons to another
niece. For this event, all of the young men came home from
their *yeshivas* and apprenticeships. The son closest to my age
was working in a pharmacy and had prospects for a position as
assistant to a doctor. We had played together as children, but
now we watched each other shyly and spoke awkwardly. When
Herschel complimented me on the embroidery of the tablecloths,
I prayed that Aunt Rifka was nearby and would think to make
me the next niece to be blessed with one of her sons. We were
young then, but wise, I think, to foresee how the decision would
be made for us anyway, and so to fall in love right then, in
preparation.

Now, you see, poverty and disease and death were ever at our doors, but we were able to survive and even have many happy times, thanks to the bonds of family and the strength of our traditions. Outcasts always, we found sanctuary in our isolation. It was as if the Jews functioned as a separate state within the various cities of Russia, and we found security within our poor but spirited communities. Our greatest misfortune was to have the Czar's regime take more of an interest in us. The attention swung between a disingenuous effort to enroll Jewish children in state schools (for the sole purpose of assimilating us), to inordinately careful census-taking (for the purpose of drafting our boys into the army). The Christian peasantry, which often lived in an even worse condition than we, was set against us, which distracted them from the inadequacies of their rulers. But there was another class of Russians also, an educated elite who returned from colleges in Europe burning with the desire to bring their country into the modern world through social revolution and industrial development. And this friendly invasion of thought was perhaps more the downfall of our *shtetls* than the pogroms and conscriptions; for instead of tightening the knot of our community where we must huddle together for safety, such new ideas loosened the weave of Jewish interdependence and we saw, as through a veil, a light from another side...

My own Herschel was one of these soldiers of enlightenment. His education among men of the medical profession opened his mind to new ideas and opened his eyes to the intractable position of the Jews under the Czar. Shy as he was with me, he was all too bold about sharing his political opinions in public. On the day he arrived at the hospital to assume his position as a physician's apprentice, the doctor informed him that the police had been around demanding to know his whereabouts. This was the day our fates were sealed, the day Herschel went into hiding.

In Russia, at that time, a man who was found to have evaded military service could be punished by death. So,

Herschel was hidden in the cellars of friends and relatives, moving from one place to the next only in disguise and only at night. Messages were passed back and forth by many a friendly hand. Really, it is incredible that an entire city could know the movements of a hundred men and boys, for at least this many were in hiding at any given time, while not a single clue was ever spilled to the police. But I tell you it was the case; this is how bound we were to one another's welfare. Still, the families of the wanted men were marked, and we soon found our businesses failing and our taxes rising.

My aunt and uncle now gave serious consideration to their son's talk of a new country, free of such persecution and full of opportunities for everyone. It was Herschel's own greatest wish, to go to the United States; now it seemed like the only possible solution for the entire family. My eldest sister eagerly assisted Aunt Rifka in the planning and preparation for our escape. She had finally been married off to an old man who had a little money which he was in the process of drinking away. Confident that my sister, the *baleboste*, could manage the groom's affairs advantageously, we all put the best face on this obvious mismatch. In our hearts we were troubled by the man's age and lack of piety. Yet a short while after her marriage, my sister confided in me that her husband was no more useless than our own father and much less trouble, since he did not always have a gaggle of schoolboys in tow. I was so shocked by her disrespect that I almost missed the point of her whole speech, which was that we were going to America, every one of the cousins and some of the aunts and uncles too, if she and Aunt Rifka had their way. Where did I fit in to these plans? Well, Herschel was the obvious candidate to be first in the New World, but Aunt Rifka would not let him go without a wife to take care of him and see that a proper household was established for those who would follow. My wish had come true; I was betrothed to my cousin Herschel.

There were numerous hurdles to overcome before this majestic plan could be enacted. Of course there was the struggle to save enough money for two sea passages and other expenses, but we were well-practiced at scrimping and took it as a matter of course. Then there was the need to find a husband for my second eldest sister so that I could be married without bringing bad luck upon my household (as if we were any strangers to bad luck!). As it happened, she had already selected a husband and was simply waiting for a time when Father would be receptive to the man's proposal. She first spoke to Aunt Rifka, who ruled over her generation as my eldest sister ruled over ours. Once Aunt Rifka had approved the match, Father's blessing was inevitable. The wedding was a thin slice of happiness in a whole plateful of troubles. I liked this brother-in-law, whose father was a fisherman and lived outside the Pale on the Baltic Sea, and who himself had served seven years in the Russian army. Aunt Rifka must have seen in him a man with the fortitude to fulfill the dream of emigration. There is no question what my sister saw in him, and I was very happy for her. I, too, would marry for love, in addition to expediency.

The greatest obstacle to our escape from Vitebsk was Herschel himself. He continued to meet with his revolutionary friends and to plant the seeds of rebellion from his various hideouts, leading to many narrow escapes from arrest. Meanwhile, two long winters had he spent in hiding and his health was deteriorating. He had to be fit for the voyage and able to pass a physical examination in order to be permitted into the United States. While his friends from the pharmacy brought him plasters and pills, I took chicken soup to him when I dared, and cried to see how thin he became. Still, he wore his jet black mustache stylishly waxed, a flag of the modern times he so longed to join, and a zest for life sparked like fire in his black-as-coal eyes. Even now, knowing all that I know, I would follow those eyes again to the ends of the earth...

It was nothing but a miracle that passage for two was finally secured for us without Herschel being discovered by the police. A wedding was out of the question. Uncle Temme even forbade the signing of papers, as officially Herschel had "disappeared" several years back. I was sent alone, by train, to Vilna. There I was finally united with Herschel, who had been smuggled out of Vitebsk by his brothers. Looking back, I think we must have had an angel at our heels keeping the police at bay, and another walking before us, smoothing the way through so many detours, checkpoints, searches and physical examinations. Somehow we made it all the way across Germany, to Bremen, where we finally boarded the ship to America. At last we were legally, if not properly, married by the ship's captain. My joy at having Herschel by my side was an antidote to the most appalling situations. What for some immigrants was a nightmarish experience, the crossing of the Atlantic, was for me a honeymoon, and a taste of the greatness of the world such as I have never had before or since. When the shores of Boston Harbor peeked through the mist, and we stood, a married couple, in the year 1899, the first of our family to set eyes on this land of freedom, I imagined us as Prince and Princess of the New World, Adam and Eve, progenitors of a new race. It gave us great pride to be the first to come to America.

Ah, children, I have been telling this story for some time and now I wish I could give it a different ending, or pretend that from this point on we are talking about some other characters, someone else's life. But you have only to look at my grey hairs and these red eyes that cry of their own accord, even when I sleep, to know that the story is mine, and mine alone. You will forgive me then, if I do not provide so much detail about the second half of my life as I have for the first...

Let us just say that five years after our arrival here, Herschel was gone and I was left with two small children, far away from my family, alone in a country whose language I could neither speak nor read.

It was my husband who knew the English, and thanks to that he had found work right away, at a hospital where he was needed to translate Yiddish for the new immigrants. The hospital and the church looked after our tenuous community, replanted in the squalid tenements of Boston's South End. Herschel, always an organizer, would find time to help the Methodist minister with distribution of the many items donated to us by that kind parish. I took care of first one baby and then two, sewed for hire and barter, and stayed generally within two Yiddish-speaking blocks of our tiny apartment. Herschel tried to teach me how to go around here and there, how to at least read the street signs, understand a couple of words... But I was terribly confused by a whole new set of letters and numbers, and by a language that had a different sound on every tongue that spoke it. I was busy enough getting to know the many dialects of Yiddish that came together here, and a little Italian, which was the first language of the neighborhood.

Could I have guessed that for not learning English I would be punished by never knowing where my husband was buried? Forgive me, children, but I did not understand then, and I do not understand now, how a man can be shown to have this "TB" and be thrown first into prison and then taken away to a sanatorium, where he cannot be loved and cared for by his own family. I saw Herschel only once after that. The train ride to the country was expensive and long and I worried the whole time about my children, who were left with a neighbor boy, just a child himself.

By the time I received word of Herschel's death, he was buried already in a pauper's plot. I think these tears will never stop, these tears that should have been wept over his grave. He is lost to us forever now, wouldn't you agree, those of you who have also searched for him?

The kind minister took me and my babies into his house and employed me to sew all of the clothes for him and his wife and their children, who were even more numerous than those of the *Chasidim* of Vitebsk. If it were not for this, I am sure we would have died.

Herschel's brothers were already on their way. My sisters followed with their husbands and children, except that my eldest sister conveniently left her drunken husband behind. Uncle

Temme, my father-in-law, was the only one of his generation to make the trip; after Aunt Rifka's death he eagerly followed his remaining family to Boston. I do not think I could have faced Aunt Rifka again, in this life, having so pitifully lost the son she entrusted to me; and I'm not sure I will be able to face her in the next. My eldest sister, the *baleboste*, took Aunt Rifka's place in the New World.

And so my story ends, strangely, as it began, with me in a house run by my sister, with our own children to provide for instead of our little siblings, and much visiting and sharing, and squabbling, among the branches of the family, and the uneasiness of being outsiders, and the constant scheming to multiply our meager resources, and the struggle to be a little healthier, a little smarter, a little braver, so that life need not be so hard...

There, there, pay no attention to these tears; you see how they make a regular appearance, like hungry relatives, and I do not know how to turn them away. Look instead at how my hands still fly when I take up the needle; and lest you think I am full of only pity and no pride, listen here: things are indeed better in America. Yes, Herschel could have been healthier, and I smarter, but none could have been **braver** than we. Because we, Herschel and I, we were the first to come.

The Dance Of The Matriarchs

Now
This dance of mine is not of the furniture filled parlors
Of Russian immigrants
(Imagine bric-a-brac, *tsatskes*, flying about
Shattering into many pieces
Sent aloft by my spinning veils and skirts and arms thrown wide)
No, this is a dance to be danced upon hard packed earth —
In open air —
By blazing firelight or beneath blistering sun
I can see my ancestors sitting around a fire under an ancient sky
Exploding with stars
They beat drums and play pipes
While aunts, cousins and grandmothers' grandmothers
Dance with me
She presides, the Matriarch
We converse

Yes, we have all had this dream

This dream which was once a memory?

Dance and dream; if it pleases you, call the dream Memory

It pleases me; and what shall I call the dance?

Mother

Some say sleep is a man who throws sand in our eyes
But I say
Sleep is a woman who dances
And every rustle of her folds of silk
And every jingle of her jewelry
Is a constellation of thoughts that swirl and undulate
Until there are so many that the mind is overwhelmed
And only dreams can contain them

Who is this dream dancer?
For me she is the spirit that links all of the women of my line
And she brings them to me as I sleep
So they may share the joys and sorrows that shaped their lives
And ultimately mine
For there is much unfinished business among my women
(Among all women)
Love inadequately expressed
Children unborn or too soon deceased
Anger denied
Work uncompleted
Wisdom rejected

Water permeates my dreams
Still waters and flowing waters
Baths, pools, ponds, streams, rivers, oceans
Often the tame water lies within or beside the wild water
A swimming pool within a sea
Like the steady heart of an obedient wife
Within the tempestuous soul of a goddess
What water shall I swim in?
The pool is safe, steady, known
The sea is black or pure blue, limitless, throbbing with life
The horizon alternately smiles and frowns beyond the waves
The pool has walls
I could be crushed against them

The sea has no end
I might be lost within it

Water permeates my dreams
Secret messages from women who came before
Seep into my pores
Wet me through with desire
Shake me with fear
Strangle me with rage
And the one who dances
Is counting out a universe of possibilities
With the soles of her feet
And another with her clapping hands
And another with the arch of her eyebrows

We are joined as one within the dream dancer's dance
The women of my line and I
For our nightly debate
Shall we swim or not?
Shall we go here or there?
Shall we wear these clothes or those?
Shall we love this man or another?
Shall we eat or fast?
Shall we run or fight?
Objects fall from the sky
Buildings crumble
Animals speak
And the waters beckon, beckon

> *It doesn't matter where you swim*
> *The waters of life are contained within*

The Black Sea

The Black Sea

Dream Journal Entry

I was in Europe for the first time, in a car with two other people: a guy, who was driving, and a young Roumanian woman. We arrived at the woman's home and walked up to the house where her mother came out to greet us. I was very excited to be there and as I looked around and away from the short row of houses I realized that the dark landscape around me was an ocean. It was the Black Sea and it was indeed black except for the whitecaps, and it was so powerful and beautiful that though I tried to exclaim over it I couldn't get the words out. Finally I was able to express my feelings of both being frightened by it and being drawn to it as if I might leap in against my better judgment. The mother and daughter looked at each other knowingly and said, "Papa will understand." I noticed then that the rows of houses were on a sort of floating boardwalk and the sea was all around them. People were in the water on the other side, where it seemed to be calmer but it was just as black. They were plump and naked and bobbed and dove like porpoises.

I Am The Em

i am the em in
woMan
part of woM(b)
part of Man
divided even within myself
a hump here
a hump   there
the customary extra
stroke
lends weight to the
woM side
she demands
I must be completely
rOund
I must know nothing less
than life and death
earth and flesh...
whereas
the Man Me
has a different Idea
of conception
and productivity
wind-powered
steam-driven
his motion is an arrow's

stroke
hump hump
i am the em in woMan

EMpty vessel
dark with mystery
propelled through Orbit at light speed
i make myself rOund
from the Outside

Di Menshen

Ever see Muddy Waters perform his old blues hit
I'm A Man
Or, as he would sing it,
Mmmmmmmmmmmaaaaaaaaaaaaaaaaayyyyyyyyyynnnnnnnnnnuuuhh

I'm A Man
He spells it out
Eeeeeeeeeeeeeehhhhhhhhhmmmmmmmmmmmmmmmmmmuuuhh
(mama)
Aaaaaaaaaaaaaaaaayyyyyyyyyyyyyyyyyyyyiiiiiiiiiieeeeeeeeeeeeehhh
(honey)
Eeeeeeeeeeeeeeeehhhhhhhhhhhhhnnnnnnnnnnnnnnnnnmmmmuuhh
(child)
Mmmmmmmmmmmaaaaaaaaaaaaaaaaayyyyyyyyyynnnnnnnnnnuuuhh

And he shakes his jowls to hold the note out even longer
Because a single syllable to sound the soul of Man won't do
The female of the species, Woman, at least gets two

120

The Tree

He is not an old man
Just a tired man who feels old
As he trudges home from a ten-hour workday
Six days a week he works
Taking only the Sabbath off
And he remembers when he had to work seven
It didn't matter then
About the Sabbath
And the old ways
To his wife, to his mother
But not to him
For whom the magic of the ritual
Had been left behind on the other side of an ocean
Along with his childhood
He is not an old man
Just one who got off to an early start
In the responsibility department

Six days a week, ten hours a day, he works
Yet still he sits long into the night
Reading and studying
As he was taught to do in his grandfather's house
Where a printing press shared residence
With the family's pet goat
He hungers for knowledge

The long days of tallying accounts
Leave him empty, numbed
As he rounds the corner to his street
Does his step quicken in anticipation
Of the hot meal on the table
Or of the paper-wrapped books expected from the postman?
Like grandmother's goat he will devour anything
Pulp novels, physics textbooks...
He belongs to the synagogue, the book club
He has his family, and, when he's lucky, a job
Yet within himself he feels alone
He needs rest, but craves the energy to do more
Work puts food on the plate
Sleep makes work possible
But work and sleep do not make a life
A good wife makes the home a palace, a sanctuary
Healthy children honor the past
Carry the family names into the future
But a man should not have to choose between
Supporting his family and enjoying their company

Here, here is his yard
The house he toils to keep
But all is not right this evening
Look, that limb still hangs dangerously from the linden tree
The men did not come as scheduled to remove it
He scowls
What's the use of laboring to keep a roof over their heads
If a heavy branch is waiting to fall on them
In their own front yard?
He straightens, invigorated
See, he is needed here
Earning a paycheck is not all that a husband does

He slips into the house

She is out
Of course, it is *Tisha b'Av*
A day of mourning and sadness
She fasted today and is at the Temple now
He sighs
I work all day for the *goyim*
And she prays all day to God
Meanwhile, Mother Nature will send this tree
Down upon our heads
Well, not if I can help it
Saw in hand, he returns to his yard and climbs the tree
And why not?
He is not an old man
In fact, he feels younger by the minute
Sawing away at the cracked limb that now looms in his mind
As an assassin
The threatening branch crashes to the ground
He remains in the tree
The long summer dusk soothing him
The cool broad linden leaves brushing his cheeks
So hot from exertion
Stars appear
He sees them as the twinkling eyes of angels
And feels blessed here in his lovely tree
His fine house awaiting his repose
His wife on her way home to him
Tonight, instead of picking up his book
He will ask her to sing to him the songs of their youth

But, descending the tree is much harder than climbing it
The day's long hours wash over him
His heart beats wildly
Between fighting the weary feeling
And rejoicing in the vanquishing of the branch
He enters the house clutching his chest

And staggers to his bed
He wants to take off his shoes but cannot
The room spins, becomes the starry sky,
A blur of linden leaves
Come, Come, the angels sing

No, no, I am not an old man, he gasps
Wait, wait

Her face
She is there
Her face one last time
Her face
Tears
I'm so sorry, my *feygeleh*, so sorry
But at least I leave you on *Tisha b'Av*
And you will not have to mourn an extra day of the year for me
Es iz bashert...
Her face
Tears
Stars
Linden leaves
The voices of angels
Come, come

The Tree

Balls And Chains

Here was a man with many talents
Particularly skills of hand.
With a pocket knife as his only tool
He could turn a broomstick into the links of a chain,
Or a set of chess pieces
Or, most mysterious of all,
A tiny cage of spiraling wooden veins
Entrapping a perfectly round wooden ball.

Here was a man with many talents
Particularly skills of hand.
And yet for employment
He was required to do nothing
But watch.
He was forbidden to read.
He was forbidden to whittle.
Only his eyes and ears were to be engaged
In constant surveillance of the prison grounds
From his idle perch in the guard tower.

Here was a man with many talents
Particularly skills of hand.
And there could not be a harsher punishment
Than to make him be still and confined.
Although he was free to go at the end of his shift,

During his time in the tower
He must have felt as trapped as any of his wards
And even envied them their books and cards and pastimes.
Perhaps he felt more kinship with the prisoners
Than with the other guards.
And at least once his quiet empathy helped avert a riot
Where another man's frustrated energies
Would have fanned the flames.

Here was a man with many talents
Particularly skills of hand.
He learned his crafts from his own father
And reading books
And working problems out for himself.
What he learned, he learned well;
But what he never learned was to do nothing.
No one could teach him this,
Not the warden or the convicts or even his family's need;
And late into his watch
He would often risk dismissal
By pulling from his pockets four inches worth of broomstick
And a pocket knife
With which to carve a tiny cage of spiraling wooden veins
Entrapping a perfectly round wooden ball.

What The Mirror Saw

Filling the wall above a tall mantelpiece, the mirror's vast surface reflected primarily air, the tops of heads, lampshades, candelabra, and the distant opposite wall of the long room. The mantel itself was maple; it stretched lustrously above an elegant lady who reclined in a clearing in a wood. She was painted on the tiles that made up the face of the mantelpiece. Below her, along each side of the hearth, were depicted two medieval musicians, lute player to the right and piper to the left. The entire composition was framed in narrow brass sheets into which the shapes of leaves and grapevines had been beaten. These were prosperous times for the man who had commissioned the mirror and mantelpiece. The back of his bald head often bobbed about in the lower periphery of the mirror's view as he held court at his hearth. He was a generous man, gregarious, and he loved to throw parties. Many a hand ungloved before the warmth of his crackling fire, many a hooped, shimmering satin skirt twirled across his polished wooden floor, many a brandy glass was set on his maple mantel. The delicate, secret perceptions of the mirror were privy to great plumes of cigar smoke wafting high above top-hats and tiaras. Ringlets bounced, feathers shivered, capes twirled. But because mirrors do not hear (as do walls) - they only see - the laughter and music and loud talking went without note, as did the frenzied sounds of the battalion of servants that swarmed over the ballroom by day. Drapes were drawn or closed, lamps lit or extinguished, the air filled with smoke or dust, light shifted, shapes shifted... this is

128

how the mirror perceived events in the long room.

The good years were followed by a bad time. War. The parties turned into rallies, dancing gave way to weeping and argument. The mirror's vision dimmed with the spirits of the room's occupants. There was less and less to look at. When the long room was eventually closed up entirely, its furniture draped, the windows shuttered, it was as if the mirror slept.

In time, after a long period of abandonment, the mansion which housed the long room with the elegant mantelpiece and the tall mirror came to be occupied by a genial heiress. Champagne and dancing were again the order of the day, and were observed by the mirror in its usual fashion. But the heiress ran through her fortune quickly, and again the windows in the long room were shuttered. This time the mirror recognized the darkness. It did not sleep. It remained alert, a single great unblinking eye adjusting to the dark, hoping to see something.

The first shape to emerge from the darkness was a spider. It dangled a few inches from the mirror and perfectly centered, as if purposefully positioned for the best view. The spider looked at itself. The mirror looked at the spider. Neither was in a hurry. After a while, the mirror looked at the thread from which the spider was suspended. It reached from the spider all the way up to the ceiling. The mirror went all the way up to the ceiling also. It could see the ceiling. Then the mirror began to notice the other shapes it dimly reflected in the darkened, draped, long room. The spider, at least, was active. The mirror followed its movements studiously, and waited, wondering if there would ever be anything more to see.

Inanimate objects are nothing if not patient, and in time the mirror was treated to some new but familiar sights: light again spilled in from the windows. Tops of heads came and went. Feather dusters swept away the spider's web. An occasional spiral of cigarette smoke curled upwards. All that was to be seen was seen by the mirror. But the conversations which would determine the mirror's fate, and the fate of the other furnishings of the mansion, echoed invisibly off its smooth glass.

Outside of the walls of the mansion of the mirror, a city
was being built. Contributing to this effort in his own small way
was a man everyone called Jack, because he knew many trades
— and he built a house.

Jack lived with his wife, May, in a neighborhood near the
penitentiary where he worked as a guard. He spent his free time
fixing up the little house he had bought cheap from a dentist who
was gradually selling off all of his family's land in that area.
When Jack worked on his house, he felt like his father. He
remembered his dad coming home from the railroad yards with
salvaged bits of glass and wood for use in their continuous home
renovations. Now, as Jack put up a porch, a garage, bookcases
and partitions, fixed the scraping doors and squeaking windows,
his memories of being a boy and helping his father with these
same tasks added to the pleasure of his work. Jack hoped he had
taught his own son as well, and missed having him there to help.
But Max was all grown up, back from the army and off again to
college. Jack wasn't sure who he missed more, his father or his
son. And when he saw that he was actually nearing the end of
the list of improvements he had planned for the house, Jack
became restive. What would he do next?

Every day Jack walked to work past a vacant lot, one house
away from his own place. He knew that the dentist owned this
property also. What would it cost, he wondered, to buy the
land? What would it take to put up a house? He planned and
calculated; his shifts at the prison went by quickly with his
thoughts turning so earnestly around this puzzle. To May, he
said nothing at first. She worked downtown all week as a typist.
Every penny of her pay was already going into the bank. She
wouldn't even buy herself new clothes. Every other night she
washed and starched and pressed the one dress that she wore to
work each day. She was already doing all she could; no sense
worrying her with these plans until the time was right.

Jack's final household project was to fix up a room for his
father. Grandpa, as he was now referred to even by his
children, was moving in with Jack and May. They gladly

received the delightful old man. Black pipe drooping out from under his drooping black mustache, hand-carved cane by his side, wool scarf around his neck, Grandpa provided a wealth of information on many subjects. His health was failing but his spirits never flagged. When Jack confided his dream of building a house, Grandpa rallied to the cause at once. He would help Jack build the house, if not with his hands, then with his wisdom and encouragement. The monthly retirement pay from the railroad was of course thrown into the pot. The old master carpenter tapped his cane on the floor and beamed with excitement. Jack checked the bank balance. Maybe just enough.

May never knew if the deal for the property down the street was a lucky coincidence or already prearranged by Jack and the dentist. She was busier than ever now, with Grandpa to care for, so she really didn't give it much thought. All she knew was that Jack wanted to build a house, there was a vacant lot for sale one door away, and it just so happened that the price was exactly the amount that was saved up in the bank. They bought the land; May sketched out a floor plan for her dream house and carefully filled out the forms for a construction loan. Jack had May's sketch turned into proper architectural plans by a draftsman who worked at the prison. The depleted bank account began to grow again; when enough money accumulated, a company could be hired to dig the foundation and lay the block footings for the new house.

In the middle of all of this working and saving and planning, Max came home! He had decided to finish his graduate degree at the local college. Jack was ecstatic. The pieces were all coming together. He had his land, his blueprints; the loan was about to be approved; he had his sage, bright-eyed father and his strong young son. May would quit her job to take care of them all, and although she and Jack would be working harder than ever, at least some of the time they would be working together. It was agreed that the project would start in earnest right after the first of the year, and everyone prayed for a warm winter. Jack had no trouble getting himself assigned to a full year of night shifts. He could work from four until midnight and have most of the day to work on the house. Max could also work in the evenings; in fact it was easier to conduct his chemistry experiments late at night when the school's laboratories were less in demand.

Before ground was even broken, Jack and Max had put up the garage where they would store their tools and lumber. Grandpa sat in a lawn chair with a blanket over his knees and observed every bit of the work. He was soon adopted by the across-the-street neighbors' cocker spaniel. If Grandpa was in his chair, the dog was always by his side. All of the neighbors took a great interest in the project, as did the various workmen and merchants whose services Jack enlisted. Over and over again Jack, May, Max and Grandpa explained how they were undertaking the building of a house from the ground up. Their scheme was greeted with a mixture of scepticism and awe, and plenty of offers of help. The man who laid the foundations left May a free load of white bricks for the barbecue she said she wanted in the backyard. Max piled them up. Now there was a garage, a foundation and an outdoor grill. Max and Jack began to put up the framing for the house itself.

Father and son did all of the carpentry work under Grandpa's watchful eye. They built the walls and the roof and the sheathing; and not a single piece of the lumber was new. Jack made the rounds of salvage yards and bought loads of used materials. The irregular boards were sorted by size and groomed for re-use. Some of the studs were so warped that they had to be slit and straightened out with wedges of wood. A spare sharpened saw blade was kept on hand at all times for cutting the nail- and resin-filled boards. The aged pine used for the floor joists was hard as steel.

As promised, the house rose from the ground up. The weather warmed and weekends found the neighborhood gathering around May's barbecue to eat and watch and help. The men hunkered down next to Grandpa's chair to listen attentively as he described the subtler details of the work. Lumber brokers drove over from across town to check on progress and drop off a free box of nails or various odds and ends they thought Jack might be able to use. There always seemed to be more food on hand when the throng left than when they arrived.

By summer, the structure was ready for a roof. This was to prove the most difficult task. First there were calculations to be made. The "hip roof," was designed to slope in from all four walls. The angles of the girders that would go from the peak of the roof to each of the four corners were checked and rechecked by Grandpa using his carpenter's square. For the construction, boards were laid across the roof girders and a sawhorse was placed on the boards. Max stood on the sawhorse and held up the ridgepole while Jack nailed the rafters to it. Once he had gotten used to his precarious position and stopped trembling, Max looked out at a panorama of the entire city stretching below. He held the ridgepole over his head, braced against the sharp, precise raps of his father's hammer.

The roof was sheathed with boards, 1"x10"s and 1"x8"s, as plywood was too expensive. Day after day, the men worked to the very limits of their endurance, with Grandpa gazing up at them, scratching the dog's ears nervously. The old man would never be able to come up and inspect the job, but Jack and Max worked for his approval anyway. Finally, on a very hot July day, with gallons of May's lemonade on hand, Max and Jack shingled the roof.

By autumn all of the walls and the inside framing were in place. Max had bought damaged fiberboard in 4′x12′ sheets and these were cut down to 4′x8′ for the walls with the 4′x4′ remnants saved for the ceiling. The plumbing and electrical wiring were installed by professionals in order to meet city code. While this work was being done, Jack and Max walled in the sunporch at May's insistence.

Jack continued to scour the city for building materials. People would tell him about buildings that were being torn down and he would go and barter for the salvage directly. He bought a whole tongue-and-groove floor of birds-eye maple this way.

It kept the men busy for months. When Jack got home from
work each night he would wind down by scraping the layers of
old wax off the flooring. He'd leave a pile of cleaned-up boards
for Max to lay, with the help of a neighbor, while he slept into
the morning. He slept easy, knowing that Grandpa would see
that the job got done right. Another of Jack's finds was the
mantelpiece he bought out of a mansion that was being torn
down across town. The brass-framed, painted tiles and maple
mantel came with an immense mirror, as wide as the mantel and
quite tall. This was carefully wrapped and stored in the garage
while the fireplace, flooring and interior walls were finished.

Max's college buddies came over and painted while on
winter break. When the job was done, Jack brought out the
great mirror. But Jack's house was not quite the same scale as
the old mansion; it turned out that the mirror was several inches
too tall to fit between the mantel and the ceiling of its new
home. A quick consultation with Grandpa and the problem was
ingeniously solved. Jack simply built out the back of the mirror
with wedges of wood so that it angled away from the top of the
wall just enough to fit perfectly in the available space. The
mirror leaned slightly forward, as if hungry to see every inch of
the spacious living room and the dining room beyond. Jack
smiled into the wide face of the mirror and the mirror seemed to
smile back. Perhaps it was an illusion caused by there being no
furniture, just freshly painted white walls, but Jack could have
sworn that for just a second he saw a long, chandelier-lit
ballroom emerge behind his own reflection. He spun around
only to see something even more impressive: his own house,
built with his own hands from the ground up. Just one year
from the groundbreaking, it was ready for occupancy.

Moving in was easy. Jack and May knew where every
piece of furniture would go. They had spent many hours
arranging paper cut-outs of furniture on May's floor plan. There
was a place for everything in the new house and spacious rooms
for Max and Grandpa. There were two bathrooms in the new
house. May's kitchen had a big cut-out wall above the sink so

that she could talk with people in the dining room while she worked in the kitchen. She could even look across into the living room and watch the brand new television set in the corner while she washed dishes. So much was new about the house and yet so much of it was old. There was an immediate feeling of familiarity and comfort about it. Around the neighborhood, there was common agreement that Jack's house was the finest on his block, both inside and out, and this was without reproach or envy. Any who had seen the effort and ingenuity that went into building the house, any who had helped, took some personal pride in the accomplishment.

The mirror thoroughly enjoyed its new, extraordinary view. Everyone who came or went through the front door of Jack's house took a peek, if not a long entranced stare, into the mirror. It learned many faces. It came to recognize the food being served on the cloth-draped table against the opposite wall. It watched games of chess being played and books being read in the soft furniture nestled beside the fireplace. It monitored the wobbly movements of a bent old man who liked to tap on the floor with his cane to see that the boards still lay tight and flat. The mirror faithfully reported the tilt of May's hat and the line of her lipstick when she readied herself to go out. It glowed romantically back into the smiles of Max and his bride-to-be. When May threw an engagement party for the couple, the mirror multiplied by two every starburst of light from her china and silver and glass. And often the mirror would see Jack come into the room and walk right up to the fireplace, slide his hand across the smooth maple mantel and bow to the reclining lady, and peer into the mirror's depths as if looking for something at a great distance. But because mirrors do not sing (as do heating vents and plumbing pipes) - but only see - the mirror could not tell the tale of its refined history; and even if it could, it would have revealed nothing of the past that was any grander than the marvelous house that Jack built.

Vandling Un Handling

Vandling Un Handling

[pronounced "vahndling ūn hahndling," rhymes with "fondling"]

Our local "Mercado" is essentially a mall of stalls. It's a big warehouse partitioned into many aisles of cubicles of assorted sizes which are rented by the month to businesses of varying degrees of formality and permanence. Everything imaginable is sold here, sometimes all in one booth. The Mercado is only open on weekends; in most cases the owners and craftspeople, with the help of family members, are personally selling their wares. Yes, much of the merchandise has a distinctly American flavor, and the whole outdoor ambience is sadly lacking, but in spirit this is truly a market like those from other times and other countries.

Hard times; poor countries. There's a feeling that everyone here is scraping along on the fringe of the system, unable or unwilling to do business on a large scale, in a more professional context. The vendors keep each other company and commiserate about the lack of sales. Everyone looks but no one buys.

There's a band playing at each corner, where the refreshments are sold. The music makes the food seem good. Banks of fluorescent lights illuminate without warmth; their flicker plays on the nerves even though invisible to the eye. There are few serious shoppers here, just people spending the afternoon seeing and being seen. Some of the clothing worn through the aisles of the Mercado puts the racks of new garments to shame.

137

At least there's an interest in clothing. But here I am trying to sell books. My great-grandparents are rolling with laughter in their graves:

> *"Books? Books! She is trying to sell books! Storybooks!"*
> *"You should sell soap. Everyone needs soap."*
> *"Herring. You could make a good living selling herring."*
> *"Sell the dairy goods; make some cheese; raise some nice chickens and sell the eggs..."*
> *"Sell them anything they want. Get yourself a little market; you could even sell a book, maybe! Ha ha ha ha ha."*
> "Wait a minute. One of you had a printing press..."
> *"And it was a good business, too. I never had to sit in the market; everyone came to me. Not like selling books!"*
> "But I wrote this book."
> *"Mazel tov. But look around you,* meydela, *they don't seem to care."*

There is a dance these browsers do through the endless aisles. Step slide, step slide, look over the right shoulder and keep the head turning until it is almost turned around backwards, but never stop, never stop. Step slide, step slide, and snap the head back around to take in the next booth just as you approach it, and repeat. Step slide, step slide, twisting back and back to the right until you've seen the whole display by the time you've walked by it and SNAP! Head back to the front and the next booth coming up, and step slide, step slide, step slide. Never stopping, passing booth after booth. Perpetual motion. Sometimes a family or several friends come by together and one looks with more interest than the others. You can see his or her head craning back and back while the companions are already on to the next display. But does the one with the light in the eye say, "Wait, look here, here is something interesting?" No, never. When the head will not rotate any further around, it is reluctantly turned forward again and the step-slide quickens for a moment to get back into tempo and the fleeting interest is gone. Today the merchants say tomorrow will be better and tomorrow they say it is only the weather or some event across town that has kept the tourists away, next week will be better.

"Listen to them. It's just the same as in our day: 'Tomorrow will be better; tomorrow will be better...' They stood in a stall and watched the world go by and said, 'Tomorrow will be better.'"

"Most of you did have better tomorrows, or your children did. Some of you did very well as grocers and salesmen."

"But we were always at the mercy of our customers. If they didn't buy, we didn't sell. There was always something out of pocket just to get started, and if you traded in perishables..."

"... you could lose your investment."

"And don't forget that we gave credit. People had to eat. Better to give some cheese away on credit than let it go bad."

"We trusted people to pay us, if not in cash then in trade."

"Really, it was a big barter system; we had a community, we had to help each other get along."

"Just like here at the Mercado. When we get tired of sitting at the booths we walk around and browse and sometimes buy things or trade with each other. We're our own best customers."

"Buying and selling is not so bad. It could be worse. But it would be better to have a craft, a meloche.*"*

"But I have one, I'm a writer and an artist."

"There she goes again..."

"For this kind of a craft the world is beating down your door?"

"At least no one can **stop** me from writing. Look, I'm writing this very minute, right here in the book booth at the Mercado. Hey, I'm writing **you**! We wouldn't be having this conversation if I wasn't writing it."

"Well, she has a point."

"Another scholar in the world!"

"A craft is a living, but art? Oy! You should go to work as a teacher."

"I guess I thought you would be more supportive..."

"You're the one taking this down. You can change it if you want."

"Sure, write down that you have fulfilled the family legacy, the hopes and dreams of your forefathers."

"That would be truth."

"You know we're very proud of you."

"But you showed up laughing."

"Honestly, we thought it was a joke."

*"Look at this market! How far we **haven't** come!"*

"And you in the middle of this whole mishegas *trying to sell books."*

"I wish you could explain it to me. What we're still doing here in the marketplace."

"And we wish you could explain it to us."

"I suppose I can try. How about this: Regardless of the setting and the circumstances, people are just people. I'm sitting here at the market just like you did and all of the generations before you because people like **stuff**. We make it, we look at it, we trade it — we write about it. Being around stuff of human creation comforts us; owning stuff makes us feel secure. As a species, we are defined by an affinity for stuff, the result of having opposable thumbs and linear thought."

"Very nicely said!"

"She has a good kup, *that girl."*

"But in our day we shopped for need, not for pleasure."

"Pleasure isn't a need, too? We needed, and we took pleasure in finding a bargain."

"The people here are not shopping for butter and eggs, but they still consider that they 'need' the black mini skirt or the howling coyote salt and pepper shakers or the Star Trek communicator pin."

"There's no accounting for taste."

"You think we didn't have our idiosyncrasies?"

"Still, I can't help feeling like I'm letting you all down, sitting in this stupid booth. You had every right to laugh."

"We can laugh because this is familiar to us, we understand it, not like some of your new ways of doing business."

"What do we know from shopping networks and money machines?"

"But listen, if this market seems primitive, maybe lower class or old fashioned, you should look again. There is no difference between you in your little stall and the executive in the big bank or fancy hotel or high-rise office. At the heart, it's all just vandling un handling, handling un vandling.*"*

"Now that's truth."

"See, we all put our heads together, we come up with the answer."

"People are just people and life is just *vandling un handling*? That's the answer?"

"That's about it."

"I couldn't put it any better."

"What about God? I thought religion was very important to you."

"Oy! Now the subject is God? Do you want to sit in this booth and scribble all night?"

"No, not really."

"Then leave it at this: Having a religion changes us, *but it does not change God. People are people and God is God. We spend our lives* vandling un handling, *our fortunes rise and fall, for which we may worship, reject or curse God; but God is unchanged..."*

"Amused, maybe..."

"Don't confuse the girl, I'm being serious here."

"Serious like God?"

"Why do you interrupt? You don't like what I'm saying about God?"

"Please! Don't argue. I think I understand: God is not humorous or serious. Those are human traits. God does not *vandle un handle*, these are human activities. People might organize their lives and their thoughts around God, what they shop for and when, but they are still just people, people *vandling un handling."*

    "This is truth."
    "I told you she had a good kup.*"*
    "And a good heart."
    "And a booth-ful of unsold books."
    "Go home, meydela, *you've done enough* vandling un handling *for one day."*
    "Thanks. Thanks for keeping me company."
    "Don't mention it.
    "Our pleasure."
    "Yes, it was just like old times."

Children Of The World

There is still one room in my family's house that I have yet to explore. I stand at the door hesitating. I know what I will find there. I do not want to go in. At every other juncture the spirits have guided me. But this room I must enter alone. Having the ancestors along will just confuse matters.

"Do you hear me? Please stay behind. I will do this, but you must wait outside. This room is mine. Perhaps we can talk about it later, but not now; this is hard enough as it is."

Just as I expected. The room is empty. The walls are bare. The floor is bare. There is not even a stool to sit on while I contemplate the vacancy. The ancestors are silent, as I requested. Nothingness. This is the room reserved for my offspring, of which I have none.

It is very quiet. It is very clean. No smells jangle my reflexes. I was worried that I might discover the spirits of my unborn children floating around. What would I do if they begged for life? But no deprived souls haunt this space. It's not so scary here. I can relax a little.

"Is anyone there? Speak up now or forever hold your peace. I'm not getting any younger, you know."

Nothing. I am alone. If I didn't know that all of those familiar rooms and loving souls waited right outside the door, I suppose this would feel depressingly lonely. But I am enjoying the coolness of the hard floor. The white walls are like four blank screens that may play any movie I want, or none at all. And if I let my mind drift, they melt away altogether. The

143

entire world rolls out before me.

> I had a dream that my lover and I lived in a house
> that had no walls. It was carpeted in grass. Furniture
> materialized as needed and then disappeared when not
> in use. Our living room consisted of a swing-set atop
> an empty mesa. Two girls approached with their
> mother and laughed to see me naked in my swing. But
> I was not the least embarrassed. I turned to my lover
> and said: "A person is allowed to be naked in her own
> house, even if the house has no walls and people can
> see in."

I feel a little foolish now, insisting that the ancestors stay
out of this. Where they're concerned, I do live in a house with
no walls. They can see in. I have feared to expose myself to
myself because I didn't want to expose myself to them. But they
reside within me. I cannot disentangle my wants and needs from
theirs.

I'm beginning to feel at ease sitting here on the bare floor
of my empty room. My obstinacy about not having children of
my own does not seem selfish, as I had feared. Lazy, perhaps,
the inevitable culmination of generations of lives lived for others,
lives lived in commemoration of the past, in persistent
determination to survive into the future. The weariness that
saps me of the energy to populate this room with yet more
offspring exudes from my genes. Surely the forebears
themselves must have sometimes repented that the brilliance of
their creativity was dimmed by worry and responsibility for
subsequent generations. I claim this silent space for them as
well as for myself. They are the inspiration for all of my artistic
and intellectual pursuits. If I refuse to be diverted by
motherhood, isn't this only because they demand more from me?

But one more thing, before I flatter myself that I am
somehow the crowning glory of our line and therefore not
beholden to extend it further: The world I live in is not the
world of my ancestors. To attempt to sustain a particular lineage

is folly in the face of a world in which the very species is threatened. The earth itself aches and sags under the weight of this teeming population that has resulted from our all-too-successful attempts at survival. Humanity is no longer served by our continuous procreation. We are crushing ourselves with our own mass and killing each other over our conflicting needs. I am not sure if I love the earth too much to burden it with still more residents, or if I hate this world so intensely that I would deprive it of the flesh of my flesh. I do know that I cherish my unborn too deeply to consign them to a future in which the value of life will be diminished by the very volume of it.

I am pacing now, overcome by a sudden feeling of claustrophobia. Is this all there is then, to live only for myself because I have no faith in the future? And whose loss is it if I have no children? The ancestors'? The world's? Only my own, I think. I hear the term "childfree" is now replacing the more negative "childless" in politically correct circles. But even for those like me who remain "childfree" by choice and not by unfortunate circumstance, there is an element of deprivation in the experience. By choice I deprive myself of fulfillment of the most basic act of existence, procreation. And while my private protest against overpopulation provides me with more mental ease, more economic freedom, more choice of lifestyle, I have this uneasy feeling that I am still somehow "less." I am less of a woman and, yes, less of a man. Because isn't caring for the family as inherent to our male tradition as to the female?

Did I say that being alone in this room didn't frighten me? It does now. For I am coming to the realization that I am not the end of just one line, but of two. Having chosen to retire the ancestral genetic material, I establish myself as some new breed of androgynous anti-procreator; and by definition, this breed also perishes with me.

The door seems to have vanished. Or perhaps it is my vision that has failed. I am not able to see the way out. It is as if I've taken myself hostage. On what terms will I surrender myself to a world I profess to despise? Not even the ancestors can bail me out of this self-imposed exile. I must negotiate for my own release or go mad. Earlier, the walls of my empty room seemed flimsy. Mirage-like, they dissolved before my eyes, replacing nothingness with the totality of life. What was that trick of mind and how can I reclaim it?

"Dream."

"Who's there?! How did you get in?!"

"Dream."

The spirits? If so, they are exercising great restraint. Except for that one word, "dream," repeated twice, I have felt that all of these thoughts were my own. I wonder, does the dream itself have a voice? Is it calling me to it? I do feel very tired, worn out from all of my pacing and thinking. Perhaps if I just lie down and close my eyes for a minute...

> A father and his daughters are looking sadly at a scene of human-caused destruction. One of the girls asks: "Won't anybody take responsibility for Nature and say that it is theirs?"

That dream! I had forgotten completely... And now the door is back! The walls are wavering in and out. I am almost back in the house with no walls. But how...?

Of course. The answer to nothingness is everythingness. It is just a matter of perspective. This anxiety I have for the planet which prohibits me from having children implies that I have not excluded myself from the concerns of humanity. Rather, I have embraced all as my own. I have taken to my breast all of the world's children, young and old. I offer as sustenance my art, which is everything I have to give. Whoever is nurtured by it I may truly call my children, and consider their works and their offspring to be my descendents as well. These walls are an illusion, forming neither prison nor defense. And one cannot be either childfree or childless when one recognizes the child within. We are all children of the world, mothers of the world, and fathers of the world. The house that we live in is the world and it has no walls. Ultimately, we each reside in it naked, exposed, but never alone.

The door swings open, a rush of air... The spirits can contain themselves no longer. They all drift in and I wait anxiously for their verdict. *"Nice room,"* someone says, *"but it could use some of your artwork on the walls."* *"How long are you going to mope around in here?"* another asks. *"Come along now, you have work to do."*

PART III

A Fable

Prelude — My Big Shoes

I hate cockroaches, despise them
They are disgusting creatures
The sight of two or three together makes my skin crawl
A swarm of four or more provokes a feeling of nausea
Would not the world be better rid of them?
What possible purpose might they serve?

They disturb my 3:00 a.m. meditations
And interrupt the messages from the spirits
With their crunching of cat food morsels
Left behind on the kitchen floor
Should I put on my big shoes
Turn on the light
And stamp out the intruders?

No, I am not inclined to go on a cockroach massacre tonight
It is not my place to kill, or even evict
These unlikable cohabitants of my world
Haven't they as much right to be here as I do?
You might say I even invited them
Leaving the crumbs unswept
And the trash pail uncovered

True, **I** pay the rent
But **they** have had to demonstrate their own kind of
Resourcefulness in order to be here with me
They've pulled themselves up from the gutter (or drain pipe)
To attain this life of comfort
This endless banquet of Cat Chow

If only they weren't so **nasty** looking...
My revulsion for them distresses me
Is speciesism any more acceptable than racism?

I have spent so many of my waking hours interpreting my dreams that I now have dreams about the dreams themselves. And so it does not surprise me that the "dream library," which started simply as a convenient title for the various book-filled rooms of my dreams, has now coalesced into a very specific setting to which I may purposefully direct my sleeping mind. Now, when dreaming, I come upon these rooms of books, my dream self says, "Aha! The Library!" In this way the dreams begin to reference each other, and sometimes cause me to wonder: Do I dream these dreams or do these dreams dream me?

So, when my dream self pauses at the shelves of the dream library, and selects a dream book, and reads a dream tale, I am forced to ask: Has my subconscious accessed material long buried in my genetic memory, or simply formatted a flight of fantasy into a familiar structure? I offer the following example:

In my dream I was descending a stair. A musty smell wafted up to me and immediately I caught sight of old leather-bound books lining the walls of the room below. I recognized "the library" and started to get that uneasy feeling that I had lost my assignment. There was a particular book I was supposed to be looking for, but I couldn't remember the title, author, or even the subject. I entered the room at the foot of the stairs and saw how it opened out onto many more rooms full of bookshelves. Making my task more difficult, my eyes were stinging and I could not read any of the book jackets through my blurred vision. I heard a scratching sound and followed it to a remote alcove where several books had fallen to the floor. Something small and shiny scurried away from one of the books and I saw that it lay open to the title page. I bent down to try to read it but I could not focus my eyes well enough to make out the letters. Determined to see, I picked up the open book and brought it close

to my face. The musty smell filled my nostrils again,
I could hear the skittering of that insect nearby, and
then my vision cleared. The little alcove had turned
into a modern library reading room, and there I took a
comfortable seat by the window and read the following
story...

The Cockroach And The Jew

I

There was once a certain notary clerk in a small but pleasant
town in the district of R. He and his family lived in a
comfortable home in a quiet neighborhood with orderly streets
and manicured gardens. Every night, after the lights were
extinguished, a variety of small creatures would take over the
kitchen and parlor of the clerk's house. First to appear would
be the mice who would scurry about the floors gathering every
stray crumb missed by the clerk's wife's broom. Next, the
resident cricket would take his place in a hollow of the intricate
gilt picture frame surrounding the portrait of the clerk's mother's
father. From these distinguished surroundings the cricket would
begin his evening serenade. Finally, up out of the kitchen sink
drain would emerge the cockroaches in a long line. They would
fan out around the counters and floorboards for a leisurely meal
of wallpaper paste.

On some nights, the cricket would chirp so loudly that the
clerk would wake up. He would stride angrily into the parlor
with his lantern and a rolled up newspaper with which to end
Cricket's song once and for all. But the clerk would never find
the silenced insect, only fat black cockroaches unlucky enough
to be caught in the pool of lantern light. The clerk would flail
away at these intruders with the newspaper until he had
exhausted himself, when he would return wearily to bed.

So this is how things were in the house of the notary clerk after dark. During daylight hours there was of course the usual bustle of the human world, but this was of little concern to those who worked the night shift.

One day the clerk's wife awoke to feel a chill in the air. She observed that the green of her summer lawn had taken on a golden tinge, and she had a sudden urge to bake. "The wood-seller should be coming around any day now," she said to the children as she studied the dwindling pile of firewood, "and you'll soon be off to school again." This did not bring cheer to the children. "But today I will bake you a cake," she said to bring back their smiles. "Hmm, I ought only to mix the batter for now; I'll have to wait until I am ready to put dinner in the oven to bake your cake, or we might run out of wood. It could get cold the next night or two." The children watched hungrily as flour and sugar, butter and eggs, cream and vanilla were stirred into a thick, sweet-smelling batter. But the stove remained cold. They all ate a cold lunch. The day grew hot, summer again, and the clerk's wife worried over her uncooked batter, peeking under the cloth that covered its bowl in between peeling potatoes and chopping carrots for that night's stew. How relieved she was when who should come to the door but the wood-seller. "Oh yes, oh yes. I can use a small bundle right away, and then you should come back again on Saturday and my husband will buy enough to fill our shed for the winter."

"But I have a full load right here, and my strong young son along to stack the wood in your shed. Won't your husband be delighted not to have to lift and carry after working so hard in his office all week long? Come now, the price is just the same for you as for your husband."

"I much prefer my husband deal with such business. Your wood is good, I'm sure, and the price fair, but what do I know of such things? My husband works just half a day on Saturday. If you bring your son again on Saturday afternoon, I will give him a piece of the cake I am going to put into the oven right now."

"Madam, you are kind to overlook my black garments and whiskers and treat me as you would a neighbor, but must I point out the obvious? I am a Jew. Saturday is our Sabbath. We do not work on Sabbath. Your shed full of wood will put a beautiful plump chicken on our Sabbath table and new shoes on the children's feet — or it won't. Even this lowly wood-seller is entitled to a day of rest and prayer. I can feast on roast chicken or have only broth; what do such things matter to a man who is nourished by faith? And as for your cake, I'm sure it will be delicious but you will understand that we cannot eat food from the kitchen of a non-Jew who does not keep our dietary laws."

The clerk's wife was mortified. There is nothing worse than feeling insulted and guilty at the same time. She was acutely aware of the round, fresh-scrubbed faces of her own children peering at the strange, bearded wood-seller from behind her skirts, and of the gaunt figure of the wood-seller's son standing in the street by his cart. She bought the full load of wood and consoled herself that her husband **would** be glad to have this chore all taken care of (she needn't tell him of the unpleasant discussion of the Jew's Sabbath). She smiled, knowing that the wood-seller and his family would be indebted to her and her big-heartedness, her Christian-ness. By the time the cake came out of the oven she was feeling very noble. When her husband arrived home, he too was pleased with her.

Now, unbeknownst to the clerk, his wife, the wood-seller and the wood-seller's son, a very unusual creature had been transported into the clerk's shed along with his load of firewood. Yes, along with the long-legged spiders, the bits of furry fungus and the winged termite ants that had clung to the logs from forest to shed, a minuscule Jew, complete with side curls and black hat and coat, and no bigger than a woman's thumb, had also stowed away amidst the bundles of wood.

So, how did the Jew get to be so minute? And what was he doing in the forest with the spiders and termites? And why did he not cry for help from the wood-seller and his son?

Certainly the Jew had once been normal size and had in fact been a wood-seller himself. Having no wife to keep the Sabbath for him, and no son to help him cut and cart his wood, the Jew had gone to the forest alone one Saturday to get a jump on the competition. Lifting his axe, he was stopped mid-swing by an unfriendly voice:

"What are you doing there? This is not your day to be in the forest!"

It was a forest gnome, not three feet high, but round and burly and **angry**.

"Little man, little man," the Jew replied, "I have heard of such men as you living in the forest, but no one ever told me you were Rabbis. What business is it of yours that I come to chop wood on the Sabbath?"

"All week I spend hiding from the likes of you. On Saturday I own the forest. I care nothing for your religion and your Rabbis, but I **won't** have you tearing up the forest on Saturday! Saturday is **my** day!"

"So, little man, little man, how do you propose to prevent me from carrying out my work?" the Jew said, lifting his axe once more.

"Little man, little man," the gnome mimicked, grinning nastily. And he threw a handful of magic dust at the Jew, who instantly began to shrink all the way down to the size of a bug.

"What have you done? What have you done?" the unfortunate Jew shrieked, jumping up and down next to his axe, which now lay on the ground like a log next to an insect. But the gnome only laughed and said, "I can't hear a word, little man, your voice is too small." And he stomped away dragging the Jew's axe behind him and laughing merrily.

What to do? Even if the Jew had been able to call out loudly enough to make himself heard by the wood-seller or his son, what then? He would be a monster to them, an aberration of nature. They might squash him there and then. Or listen to his story and find no grounds for mercy. Chopping wood on the Sabbath? The gnome was obviously an angel of the Lord and had doled out the appropriate punishment. At best the men would run off in awe and terror and spread word that a part of the forest was cursed so that none would go there for a full season or more, and the miniature Jew would be left to be eaten by birds or die of cold. No, his only hope was to clamber aboard a freshly felled and cut log and hope to make it to a *goyisha* home where he could — what? Here he had made it as far as the woodshed, but again, what to do?

What indeed! The Christian community was as superstitious, if not more so, as the people of the *shtetl*. A miniature man, of any race, was certain to be looked on as a bad omen. And even if they did not kill him outright, who would dare to intervene with the forest gnomes on the behalf of a faithless Jew? Still, staying in the woodshed meant eventual death by cold or starvation as surely as remaining in the forest. "I have lived this long," the Jew said, brushing the wood splinters from his coat, "which is another miracle. I could have been crushed a hundred times already, between rolling around in that cart and being tossed into this shed while clinging to a bundle of logs. So, God, you punish me, but you do not kill me. Well, I am ready for your next miracle."

The Jew was in surprisingly good humor. It had been four days since the spell of the gnome had been cast. Such a little body required very little in the way of food, and the Jew had lasted on the crust of *challah* he had in his coat pocket and some wild blackberries - over-ripe, like sweet wine - he had found fallen beneath their brambles in the forest undergrowth. In fact, once the immediate terror of being turned into a virtual insect had subsided, the Jew began to think of his situation as more of a holiday in the country than a dreadful, possibly deadly, prank. What a pleasure not to have to toil all day! The ripe blackberries were food and drink combined and the mulch of leaves on the forest floor exuded a moist heat that kept one warm at night better than any blazing hearth.

So, the Jew had survived the forest. But the woodshed of the notary clerk was going to be more difficult. The bundles of wood had been stacked so high and so deep that even the one sliver of light which might have made its way under the cockeyed door had nowhere to go. The shed was black as night and smelled of fungus.

II

In the woodshed of the notary clerk, the Jew perched uncertainly on the side of a mountain of firewood and suggested again that he was ready for the next of God's miracles.

"Well, what do you think, my good Lord? Will you have some more fun with me or is this to be the end? Just another dead bug that couldn't make it through the winter — is this what's in store for me? I cursed your name, I admit, when I went to the forest on *Shabbes*. I said, 'Curse your day of rest! You make us a despised and impoverished race with this so-called day of rest! Every week we work our fingers to the bone and then we take a day off while our Christian neighbors fill their pockets, buying, trading and laughing all the way home...'"

"The Christians have their day of rest also. So why is the Sabbath such a particular burden to you?"

"What is that?! Who is that?! God, is that you?! If it is, you don't sound so good."

The Jew, unable to see anything or anyone in the dark shed, wasn't sure if he would be more frightened if the voice was God's or wasn't. If it wasn't, what could it be? God was supposed to have a booming voice, but this one was tinny and clipped, the sound of breaking plates. As seconds passed without response, the Jew's terror turned to disappointment, and then back to terror again as a clicking, scratching, scrambling, dust-raising presence approached over the unseen terrain of logs.

"Baruch atah adoshem..." The Jew began to say his prayers, certain that he was now to meet his end in the jaws of a rodent. He swayed and bobbed in a sudden frenzy of piety.

"**Now** listen to him. Begging for mercy. Say there, how did

you get to be so small? I know a Jew when I hear one." The
creature's crunching approach had slowed and then stopped one
long tentacle's length from the Jew.

"*Oy!* What are you? What...? Do you stab me with horns?
The Devil, you are! Such a stink! *Feh! Feh!* Get away from
me!" This as the creature probed gently, its rigid, whip-thin
whiskers intertwining with springy coils of beard.

"A Jew, a Jew, a Jew! Smaller even than I, and all his sense
shrunk too! Surely you don't think that if I was the Devil I
would choose to go around as a cockroach?! And if your God
would make you bug-size just for breaking the Sabbath - I
presume that's what all of this is about - what is to fear from the
Devil?"

"A cockroach? A talking cockroach? A talking,
philosophizing, reeking cockroach? Pew! Back off a little bit,
won't you? And tell me if it was God or the Devil that gave you
voice?" Despite the stench, the Jew found he was happy for the
chance to converse. He had felt many times in the past week
that his death was imminent, yet for another moment still his life
was spared. "All my life, I have prayed for a miracle. Now,
here I am living in a world of miracles, and I tell you, it does
not smell so good."

"Fie on you! Do you think your smell is pleasing to me?
You could use another week under the mulch pile. Here we are,
with only each other to talk to, and you insist on insults. *Feh,*
yourself! The wood-seller's whole load could not break my
back, but that tongue of yours pains me!"

The Jew sensed the cockroach backing off and heard it turn
around. Obviously, it could find its way in the dark and climb
over the logs at any angle without falling.

"Ay, me! Is there any creature on the planet I do not
offend? Why, oh Lord, do you not put an end to my miserable
being, already?"

"That God of yours will kill you yet, if you continue to
moan and babble like an idiot." The clacking voice was growing
fainter. "Or follow me into the clerk's house and live a little

longer. Tonight's the night I move in for the winter."

"Follow you? I am blind in this place."

"My smell, follow this smell you hate so much, you..." And the cockroach's voice became indecipherable under the noise of six legs retreating down the mountain of firewood.

Alone again, feeling more alone for having so recently had company, the Jew now reconsidered his willingness to perish. He began to gingerly work his way over and down the logs, following the garbage pail scent of the cockroach. It was a bruising journey, for the Jew had been granted only the size of an insect and none of its agility. Scraped and aching, he finally stumbled down to the very floor of the shed, where a slice of waning daylight peeked under the door. At the light's edge rested the cockroach, now visible to the Jew.

"*Oy gevalt!* Here my nose is just getting used to this sten... uh, smell of yours and now it is my eyes who must find tolerance for your ugliness. Forgive me, Mr. Cockroach," he hastened to add, frozen in mid-descent just above the shed floor at the sight of an insect fully twice his size. "This is such a grave shock to me. Never have I been so close to one of your species, seen you in such detail. Of course I saw some fearsome things in the forest, but nothing to match your size — were I still a full-sized man, even then I would remark upon it!"

The cockroach twitched its whiskers and appeared to preen a little bit, making it seem more human to the Jew, and less frightening. The Jew dropped to the ground just at the edge of the doorsill and gratefully inhaled the late autumn, late afternoon breeze sweeping through the crack. Now he was face-to-face with the cockroach. "So? What's the plan? Won't you talk to me now that I can see you? Tell me, can all cockroaches talk?"

At last the cockroach was moved to respond: "The older you get, the smarter you get. The smarter you get, the older you get. The older you get, the bigger you get. The bigger you get, the louder a sound you can make. The older and smarter and bigger and louder you get, the more likely you will learn to speak. Hence, one who has lived to be as large as I, has not done so without learning a trick or two. I winter under the clerk's stairs, stay out of all drain pipes, keep to the shadows and don't let myself get too greedy. So, season in and season out, there I am listening to all of the doings of the household. By Spring, my fascination with human ways has worn off, my patience with their prattle thin. And just in time, as the woman commences this great annual sweeping, scrubbing and airing of the house, I scurry over here to the shed to spend a quiet summer; I have a little route under here and right around to the slop pile."

The cockroach glowed with pride and the Jew provided a sincere display of awe. "So, you have lived this way for many years. Long enough to learn many things, including how to talk! *Mazel Tov.* Do you know how old you are?"

"Don't know, exactly, but I remember being in the house the year in which their second brat was born. Never forget that. Almost went down the drain that year. The child was sick and all the time they were washing and boiling and boiling and washing. Won't even go near a basin anymore, I won't. No, sir."

"And I presume you wait for the sun to go down before you cross to the house." The Jew was reminded of his own fragile situation.

"That's right. So you might as well lie down there in the sun and rest up. I know you humans like sun. Uugggghh!" The cockroach shuddered and shrank back at the mere thought. The Jew accepted the invitation gratefully and stretched out on the warm wooden doorsill. He could have rolled right under and out into the yard there and then. Instead, he fell instantly asleep under the watchful eye of the cockroach. He had no dreams. The sun set; the breeze turned chill. The Jew awoke clear-headed at the sound of the cockroach's clacked, "Now, go!"

III

"Now, go!"

And the Jew rolled out into the night. The cockroach followed, unhurried, while the Jew stood and brushed off his coat and pants. He was running fingers through his beard, plucking out more wood splinters, when his guide came close and examined him curiously.

"What are you doing?"

"I want to look like a decent, normal - well, except in size - man when I ask the clerk for his help."

"You're not serious! He will squash you underfoot, or with his newspaper. Might as well freeze out here!"

"Well, I do have some fears in that regard, but I've decided to put them aside. I am a man, a decent man, even with my recent transgressions. The clerk is a decent man too, even if he is a *goy*. Won't he, like you, be curious? Won't he, like you, extend a helping hand to one in need? Surely if you - forgive me for saying so - a mere insect, can have such compassion for one such as I, will not one of my own kind show even greater concern?"

"You have the mind of an infant! The clerk will not see you as his own kind. Perhaps as a demon, a sprite, a little Jewish devil, but more likely as just another bug like me. With your black coat and your black hat and your little voice that he cannot even hear, why, you are more like me than him. **Now** I'm not sure I should take you into the house at all. You will get us both killed. And tell me, what possible thing could the clerk do to help you, besides keep you as a pet, or sell you to the circus?"

"I was thinking more along the lines of someone taking me to the Rabbi to see if he might have a Word that will make me grow back to my normal size. But why be choosey? I would just as willingly let one of their priests have a try. After all, there's no telling what faith is practiced by those little men of the forest."

Making a sound the Jew had not heard before, but rightly
interpreted as one of disgust, the cockroach started off toward
the house. He let the Jew follow, but did not invite further
conversation. The two small shadows slithered unnoticed
through the roots of brown-tipped grasses.

Getting into the clerk's house was as easy as getting out of
the shed. The gap under the kitchen door was slight, but still
afforded sufficient clearance for both large insect and small man.
A whiff of dinner still lingering in the air set the Jew's stomach
to rumbling.

"Dear God, what a trial you have prepared for me," he
muttered. "Even if I should find a pitiful crumb in the cracks of
the floor, it could be *tref*. Off a Jewish floor I would eat, but
this... Hmmm, perhaps by day I can watch what they eat and
hope for a morsel of something *pareve* to fall to the ground."

"What's *pareve*?" In spite of himself, the cockroach was
intrigued.

"Something that is neither milk nor meat, that is naturally
kosher, like fruit and nuts." Another loud protest from the Jew's
stomach drew curious looks from some other insects grazing
throughout the kitchen, now faintly illuminated by the light of
the moon. Their presence unsettled the Jew but was archly
ignored by the king cockroach. The latter was now viewing the
former as something of a pet. Gesturing with his antennae for
the Jew to follow, the cockroach led the way across the parlor
and into a deep, dark alcove beneath the stairs.

Once engulfed in darkness, the Jew stood still and listened
as his companion scrambled and chewed and probed, surveying
their surroundings. After a short while the cockroach called to
the Jew, "Follow me now, my voice or my scent if you can, I've
found some dried pears for you; must be last year's. I bet the
people have forgotten about them."

Eagerly the Jew picked his way after the cockroach, climbing
up the side of a burlap bag and then almost falling through the
hole the insect had chewed through the fabric. He plunged his
hand in and broke off a piece of sweet, dry pear. As it softened

in his mouth, the Jew wondered what other delicacies were stored below the stairs and looked forward to making his own investigations by day. Hearing the cockroach stir and move off, the Jew remembered his manners. "Thank you, Mr. Cockroach, you are a real *mensh.*"

"You're welcome, I think. Now, if you will excuse me, I am off to get a bite to eat myself. Stay put there and beware of spiders."

Engulfed yet again by terror, the Jew chewed worriedly on his dried fruit, straining to hear whatever sound a spider might make. But fear-induced exhaustion overtook him and soon he dozed, drooling pear juice into his beard while the sound of a solitary cricket filled the night.

Being a tiny creature, the Jew now slept and woke many times during the course of a single night and day. Sometimes when the Jew woke he was full of fear, sometimes hunger, sometimes curiosity, and sometimes all three. Sometimes the mammoth cockroach was near at hand, friendly and talkative, and sometimes he was nowhere to be found. The Jew learned how to fend for himself and concentrated on the doings of the notary clerk's family, looking for an opportunity to plead his case to them. He concluded that he would make his appearance by day, when he was less likely to be mistaken for an insect or overlooked entirely, and that he would wait for two more nights to pass before attempting to reveal himself to his hosts. By his calculations it was now *Shabbes* eve. It would not do on the morrow, the Jewish day of rest, to have the clerk running to the Rabbi for favors. No, he would wait until Sunday, when this gentile family would be comfortably assembled in the parlor, to emerge from the shadows beneath the stairs. But, then...? What would he say? How should he draw their attention?

The Jew dozed and woke, dozed and woke, dreaming and thinking of the speech he would deliver to the notary clerk. The cockroach, sensing his friend's preoccupation, did not intrude on the Jew's thoughts. When the moment of truth finally arrived, the great insect was deep in hiding...

The Jew arranged his soiled clothing, smoothed his beard, and strode out into the light of the parlor. There sat the clerk and his wife quizzing the youngest son on his lessons. 'How like a Jewish household it is,' he thought. 'Surely they will have compassion for me.'

He walked farther and farther toward the center of the room, gaining confidence. Yet just as he was preparing to call out at the top of his lungs, the boy did so first. "A bug! A giant bug!" he shrieked, pointing a shaky finger at the Jew. As the family flew into a frenzy of disgust and outrage, the clerk booming profanities, his wife sobbing, the Jew turned with hands over his ears and ran back to the dark safety beneath the stairs. The clerk's huge boot missed him by only a hair; the breeze of it propelled him just ahead of a wildly flailing roll of papers. The Jew wedged himself into a crevice of old wood, panting, heedless of spiders. Nothing could be as terrifying as that mad giant of a man and his squalling kin. And yet, he mused, what was it that enraged them so? Nothing, if not their own terror. "For even if I was a 'damn nervy bug,' how could I possibly hurt them?"

The family still sputtered and fumed. Other children ran in from their play and were hysterically informed of the great travesty that had transpired. At the high-pitched instruction of their mother, the children used brooms to prod and poke about in the space beneath the stairs.

"See, their hearts are not really in this. They don't want to find me at all. Small and helpless as I am, they are just as afraid of me as I am of them." This gave the Jew something to think about as he anxiously awaited nightfall. He would tell all to the cockroach. They might have to move now, for the clerk's wife was threatening to give the storage space a thorough cleaning in the morning.

The cockroach did not need to hear the story from the Jew. He had already overheard the excitement in the parlor, as it had awakened him mid-day. When the family was safely in bed, he gleefully scolded the Jew. "Now will you believe me when I tell you that if you look like a bug you'll be treated like a bug? It doesn't matter who you are inside. No one wants to know about you personally. How long it would take to judge every creature on its own merits! Even if you appeared to them as a **full**-sized Jew, you would still be a Jew! Would not they still recoil in horror? You seem to have an exceedingly simple mind, not what I expected, Jew."

"Obviously, I am not a very good Jew or I would not be in this mess now! And I am not smart, either, I admit. But I could become smarter, like you. You say some very wise things, friend cockroach. I think it is time for me to resign myself to my fate. I will rest and contemplate the nature of the universe from this peculiar, puny perspective. But, do you think we will be all right here? Will they continue to hunt for us?"

"I expect the clerk will be prowling around more often than usual for the next night or two. Nothing to worry about if you stay back here and keep quiet."

"I'll do whatever you say from now on," the Jew said, trembling anew at the peril just passed.

"Gevalt!" said the cockroach.

IV

After his failed attempt to make contact with the clerk, the Jew retreated to his favorite niche and kept quietly to himself for three days and three nights. Only once during that time did the cockroach interrupt the Jew's deep meditation. It was to ask a favor for the cricket.

The cockroach wanted the Jew to give the cricket his jacket so that it too could survive the cold winter. Despite the warmth of the house, the cricket was becoming stiff and weak. The cockroach had always liked the autumnal song of a cricket in the house, and would miss the music come winter. "Until you came, I had no friend who even had a chance of lasting the winter," the cockroach admitted.

"What about your own kind?" asked the Jew. "You've got even more relatives than me!"

"Humph! They're not my kind any longer. None of them can talk, after all; at least none that I've found."

"Listen to you! I must think this all through. One thing at a time. What is a man? What is a Jew? What is a bug? And now, what is a talking bug?"

"But the cricket..."

"Yes, and should a cricket have a coat? To think that once the most serious question I ever contemplated was whether to chop the tree on the north side or on the south!"

"But the cricket..."

"No! I have decided; like that, I have decided! I have not done all this thinking for nothing. How could my coat possibly save that cricket? It is fate! A cricket doesn't live but a season. This is nature. A cricket doesn't wear clothes. It is nature. You would cheat nature? I think it is impossible. I would give the poor creature my coat and do you know what would happen? He would not be able to carry its weight. He could not hide high on the wall; he would limp along the floor. Yes, along the floor, and, with my black coat draped atop him, he would look like... me! Or... you! And then what would happen? SPLAT! Down comes the clerk's shoe and your friend dies a ghastly cruel death instead of a peaceful natural one."

The cockroach's antennae quivered in irritation. "I don't believe it is in the nature of the cockroach to speak, either," he said. He then turned his hulking shell around and left the Jew to even more intense cogitation.

The cockroach did not visit with the Jew again after that, and the Jew seemed oblivious to all around him. It was as if his body, so small already, had almost ceased to exist. He now inhabited a world of ideas. He was literally lost in thought; so lost, that one day he almost didn't notice the voice of a fellow wood-seller at the front door. When the familiar intonations finally filtered through the Jew's awareness, the clerk's wife was already sending the man on his way.

"...now, get on with you and don't come around again! I bought that wood from you last week; why would I have had business with any other wood-seller? If this friend of yours has gotten lost in the woods, it's nothing to me. I suppose the man's in trouble. Well, if he is, go talk to my husband at his office; don't come around here..."

They **had** missed him! They were out looking for him! The Jew sprang from his hiding place under the stairs and ran through the parlor and out the front door, past the feet of the clerk's wife and the wood-seller. As he ran, he cried out at the top of his lungs the thoughts that had been running through his mind for days on end. With each silent recitation of his ideas, they had become more complete, and now, as he ran to the middle of the yard and stood shaking his tiny fists at the heavens, the words that spewed forth became a prayer so complete that the angels amplified the Jew's voice so that all could hear. And yes, the Jew then began to grow. As the wood-seller and the clerk's wife, and soon all of the neighbors on the notary clerk's street and all of the merchants making their deliveries amongst them, stood watching and listening in awe, a marvelous voice came out of nowhere and was soon followed by the embodiment of a dusty, smelly Jew with a wildly unkempt beard. It was a fearful event, and some clasped their hands and implored heaven for mercy, even as did the Jew himself.

"...for is not a Christian a *goy*, and a *goy* a man, and a man a *mensh*, and a *mensh* a Jew? And therefore are not Christian and Jew one? And if you should treat the Jew like an insect, something lowly, are not then all men demeaned? Because if a Christian is a *goy* is a man is a *mensh* is a Jew and the Jew is an insect; then the Christian is an insect too. And in any event, who is entitled to be insulted by this? The Jew? The Christian? I think not. It is the insect who ought to be insulted. To be compared to a man! What have we to show for all of our strength and wit, I ask you? Are we masters of anything more than cruelty and greed? Ah, but it is not in the insect's nature to be insulted. And this is only one way in which he is superior to us.

"Oh, leave my body the size of a cockroach, if only my soul might continue to grow. I have learned that the spirit is a mighty thing and is not impeded by its homely shell. I...I..."

The Jew saw he had an audience, and then that he had returned to full size. He could not go on with his speech and stood bewildered, blinking in the sun. The wood-seller started to move cautiously toward him and then turned with a start as the clerk's wife let out a shriek. A great cockroach was lurching out of her front door, emerging from the shadows. Its progress was agonizingly slow despite the furious motion of its six legs. As the woman clutched her skirt and leapt backwards into the house, the wood-seller lifted his black boot.

"STOP!" the Jew bellowed, raising his hand.   The wood-seller's foot hovered in the air; a collective breath was held. The cockroach moved purposely in the direction of the Jew and did not stop until it had actually climbed atop his left boot. Then the insect's black shell seemed to melt into the dusty leather of the Jew's boot, and a moment later it was as if the entire episode had been an illusion.

But the Jew was real enough. His friend, the wood-seller, shook off the strange spell that hung over the notary clerk's street. "Come along, already. Get in my cart. If these people didn't think you were some kind of prophet, they'd be pelting us with rocks. Look, they grow agitated. Soon they'll think we've pulled some kind of hoax on them. Maybe you have done just that, friend. You and your cockroach! Come along, prophet, I am taking you straight to the Rabbi."

It was not long before the Rabbi had heard the story many times over and, across town, the same was true for the Pastor. Both were deluged with questions about the meaning of the remarkable events on the notary clerk's street. From house to house and shop to shop, arguments arose as to whether these had been holy or unholy doings. Each clergyman settled the disputes brought before him with firm instructions that the lowly Jew was to be treated with respect and generosity. For whatever reason, he had been chosen by God to bring this message of tolerance to their community. And it was not too long before the little doorstep in front of the Jew's little house became a place where men and women of all faiths, stopping to leave a basket of bread or a tureen of soup for the local prophet, would exchange friendly words with each other. Town and townspeople flourished, and the Jew never again had to go out and chop wood to earn money to buy his bread. But it should be noted that the charity of the Jew's benefactors did not extend to social visits with the prophet himself. For naturally the Jew was feared for his mystical powers. While many were willing to contribute gifts of food and clothes and firewood, even the Jew's oldest friends now felt uncomfortable in his presence. It seemed that everyone stopped at his door but no one went in to visit. But this is only how it seemed.

In truth, the Jew had two regular visitors. They came only at night and never together, for they were none other than the Rabbi and the Pastor! There was even a secret schedule whereby the Rabbi would make his visits on Sunday and Tuesday evenings and the Pastor his on Mondays and Wednesdays. Understanding the Jew to be specially blessed by God, these two spiritual leaders would go to him regularly for advice. Whether perplexed by difficult questions posed by their congregants, or uncertain as to how to interpret a sacred text, the clergymen were never disappointed with the guidance they received in their sessions with the poor Jew. And if they sometimes noticed that the Jew crossed his left leg over his right and leaned far, far forward, as if listening to his boot, they simply attributed this to the idiosyncrasies of a wise man.

The End

The Dream Library

Glossary Of Foreign Words And Phrases

Baruch atah adoshem (Heb.) — the first line of a prayer, lit. "Blessed be the name"

baleboste (Yid.) — housewife, manager, bossy woman

Bobe (Yid.) — grandmother

challah (Heb.) — a braided egg bread

Chasidim (Heb.) — members of an orthodox sect of Judaism

Es iz bashert... (Yid.) — It is fate

Feh (Yid.) — Yuk

feygeleh (Yid.) — little bird

gelt (Yid.) — money

Gevalt (Yid.) — a cry of fear, astonishment, amazement

goy, goyim, goyisha (Yid.) — non-Jew, non-Jews, non-Jewish

kibitzer (Yid.) — one who meddles

klutz (Yid.) — bungler

kosher (Heb.) — per Jewish dietary laws

kup (Yid.) — head

Mazel Tov (Heb.) — Congratulations

Me'a Shearim (Heb.) — name of a 19th-century Jewish settlement in Old Jerusalem

meloche (Heb.) — craft, skill

mensh (Yid.) — a human being; a decent, honorable man

meshugenah (Yid.) — crazy

meydela (Yid.) — girl

mishegas (Yid.) — madness, silliness

mitzvah (Heb.) — good deed

naches (Yid.) — blessings; pride plus pleasure

Nu (Yid.) — So

Oy (Yid.) — Oh (all-purpose exclamation)

Oy gevalt (Yid.) — sort of like, "for heaven's sake"

Pale (of Settlement) (Eng.) — area of 19th-century Russia in which the Jews were confined by law

pareve (Yid.) — neither meat nor dairy

pogroms (Eng.) — organized attacks on the Jews in Czarist Russia

pupik (Yid.) — belly-button

Rebbe (Yid.) — Rabbi

seder (Heb.) — the traditonal Passover feast

Shabbes (Heb.) — Sabbath

Shema Yisroel (Heb.) — a Hebrew prayer, lit. "Hear O Israel"

Sholem (Yid.) — Peace; Good-bye; Hello

Sheyna meydelach (Yid.) — pretty young girls

sheytl (Yid.) — wig

shlepping (Yid.) — carrying (something heavy or awkward)

shmaltz (Yid.) — rendered fat

shtetl (Yid.) — Jewish community

Shul (Yid.) — synagogue

tichel (Yid.) — kerchief

Tisha b'Av (Heb.) — Ninth day of Av (on Hebrew calendar)

tref (Yid.) — non-kosher

tsatskes (Yid.) — knick-knacks

vandling un handling (Yid.) — buying and selling, trading

Yad VaShem (Heb.) — name of the memorial to the Holocaust victims in Jerusalem

yeshiva (Heb.) — Hebrew school, house of study

Available from Amador Publishers

* 8" x 10" **color** laser prints of Zelda Leah Gatuskin's original collage illustrations for ANCESTRAL NOTES, mounted on 11" x 14" mat boards. $12.50 each, plus $3.00 shipping per order.

* actual image size varies somewhat

To order send a copy of this form with payment to:

AMADOR PUBLISHERS
P. O. Box 12335
Albuquerque, NM 87195

Title	Quantity
Death Is A Wall	_____
From One End Of Time To The Other	_____
Taking The Sword	_____
Sacred Space	_____
Hair	_____
The Black Sea	_____
The Tree	_____
Vandling Un Handling	_____
The Dream Library	_____

Total Prints Ordered	_____ x $12.50	_____
Copies of THE TIME DANCER	_____ x $10.00	_____
Copies of ANCESTRAL NOTES	_____ x $10.00	_____
	Shipping	3.00

TOTAL, enclosed _____

A Novel
of Gypsy Magic

Zelda Leah Gatuskin

THE TIME DANCER:
A NOVEL OF GYPSY MAGIC
by Zelda Leah Gatuskin
ISBN: 0-938513-12-5 [245 pp. Paper $10]

A romantic tale of time travel, mistaken identities and parallel worlds. Can one really navigate the sea of time? When George Drumm falls in love with the Gypsy Esmarelda, he must learn the secrets of the Spiral Map of Time, or lose her to the future. But the Gypsy is on her own quest. The two leapfrog across the Spiral in search of lost cats, missing satchels and each other, and in the process share glimpses of their magical universe with the residents of the dusty town of Caliente, in the Alternate World.

Novelist and mixed media artist, Zelda Leah Gatuskin, resides in Albuquerque, NM. THE TIME DANCER draws on her work with mandalas and symbols as well as her study of ethnic dance.

"A twisted, clever, spellbinding tale for the 1990's. Gatuskin creates a vivid and bizarre universe, certain to satisfy the appetite of enthusiasts of such authors as Lewis Carroll and J.R.R.Tolkein." — Michael Bush, Associate Artistic Director
MANHATTAN THEATRE CLUB, New York City

"Gatuskin weaves a delightfully magical story, which tricked me into thinking she was from another time, or maybe a Gypsy in a past life. I'll never look at my cats the same again." — Lisa Law, author, photographer, producer, director
FLASHING ON THE SIXTIES

"THE TIME DANCER is a delightful story — full of quest, high spirits, memorable characters and thought-provoking ideas. Gatuskin takes an intricate premise, time travel, and makes it clear, believable and focused."
— Suzanne K. Pitré, playwright and author

"I am intrigued. I find particularly fascinating her use of certain shapes to travel time, since these shapes are the foundation of this deeply spiritual dance form. As a teacher of Belly Dance and its esoteric significance, I would highly recommend that my students read this magical tale." — Swari Hhan, author
BEYOND THE EROTICISM OF BELLY DANCE:
BELLY DANCE AS SACRED DANCE

HUNGER IN THE FIRST PERSON SINGULAR
STORIES OF DESIRE AND POWER
Michelle Miller
ISBN: 0-938513-15-X [170 pp. $9.00]

A ghost town hermit desiring renewed human contact begins a journal to record her four years in isolation. A man (her animus?) appears, leaving mysterious and puzzling clues to his presence, and initiating a strange courtship which compels the woman into a profound and bewildering journey of mind, body and spirit.

Subterranean encounters between the sexes move across contemporary American city and desert landscapes.

Michelle Miller is a writer and editor, and an award-winning playwright. She lives in Albuquerque, New Mexico.

WINNER! Zia Award [BEST BOOK by a New Mexico woman writer, 1992]   -- NEW MEXICO PRESS WOMEN

"Michelle Miller goes where woman has not gone before. She has the guts and the imagination to ask our most dangerous questions. Read her -- you won't ever feel as alone again."
                                        -- Sharon Niederman, Arts Editor
                                        THE SANTA FE REPORTER

"Miller's narrator speaks spontaneously in a range of emotions we can feel, hear and experience -- anger, loneliness, humor, longing. Miller crafts a seemingly fantastic experience into one of startling reality, one that dares us to look at our real hungers as women in a world that so readily accepts masks. In these stories, which all deal with some aspect of our instinctual urges, the reader has the opportunity to experience a similar hunger, a "hunger for anything that might happen between people without masks or ritual or fear."
                                        -- BELLES LETTRES

"This is a power piece that goes straight for your emotional and sexual jugular. Miller is an emerging major talent who has here penned that combination of biography, short story and novel all into one trip that examines desire and the need for power. Male and female and place come together.   -- BOOK TALK, New Mexico Book League

"Michelle Miller is a high risk writer. She is an experimentalist of the Joyce Carol Oates school, who gambles and gambles big... And when her risks do pay off, they pay big... The personal element given to the story by this confessional diary approach makes it interactive in the strongest sense, trapping the reader in a net of interest.
                    Eva von Kesselhausen, SMALL PRESS REVIEW

A WORLD FOR THE MEEK
A FANTASY NOVEL
by H. G. Z. Willson
ISBN: 0-938513-01-X [192 pp. $9]

A post-blast life-affirming fantasy, in which the lone survivor finds a baby in the kiva, rears him, loses him, goes Zen-crazy walking from Duke City to the Gulf of California, where he survives a very long time, and finds love and meaning among the dolphins and the octopi. When the dolphins find our Noah, they think they've found a fossil.

This fantasy novel is more in the tradition of *Gulliver's Travels* and *Robinson Crusoe* than the modern interplanetary invasion and star war craze. Here sensuality and curiosity have replaced violence and acquisitiveness. Willson is also the author of *This'll Kill Ya,* a modern anti-censorship fantasy romp.

"Magically written, and full of wisdom."　　　-- BOOKS OF THE SOUTHWEST

"...a magical flower of fantasy...eerie...transcendent. As we contemplate the very real prospect of a devastating near future, Willson's daring meditation through the destruction and out the other end is a wonderful affirmation. It is also an unusual and delightfully rendered story."　　　-- SMALL PRESS REVIEW

"...very readable...really entering a world where the ego is transcended."
-- Northrup Frye, author & critic, UNIVERSITY OF TORONTO

"This wistful and eloquent book rivals Miller's CANTICLE FOR LEIBOWITZ. The devastated southwest landscape, and his subsequent idyll on the shores of the Pacific, are both compelling and vivid. This is speculative science fiction at its most tender and hopeful -- and fun to read, too."
-- Gene H. Bell-Villada, author & critic, WILLIAMS COLLEGE

"Willson combines mythic material from several traditions: the Biblical Apocalypse, Native American wisdom, and flashes of Zen Buddhism."
-- THE BLOOMSBURY REVIEW

"...original and fascinating, surprising and uplifting at once...an exercise in modern mythology, creating something grounded in our world and yet speaking to our problems on a more symbolic level...a good tale about the art of living."
-- FACT SHEET FIVE